THE WAY OF THE
WARRIOR

THE WAY OF THE
WARRIOR

THE WAY OF THE SAMURAI
INAZO NITOBE

THE ART OF WAR
SUN TZU

THE BOOK OF FIVE RINGS
MIYAMOTO MUSASHI

SIRIUS

All images courtesy of Shutterstock

SIRIUS

This edition published in 2024 by Sirius Publishing, a division of
Arcturus Publishing Limited,
26/27 Bickels Yard, 151–153 Bermondsey Street,
London SE1 3HA

ISBN: 978-1-3988-4474-2
AD011746UK

Printed in China

Contents

Introduction

This volume brings together three of the most important works on strategy ever written: *The Art of War* by Sun Tzu, *The Book of Five Rings* by Miyamoto Musashi and *The Way of the Samurai* by Inazo Nitobe. Spanning three very different environments – 6th century BCE China, during its chaotic Spring and Autumn period, 17th century Japan, in the early years of the Tokugawa Shogunate, and late 19th century Japan, following the Meiji restoration – these classic texts nonetheless find common ground in highlighting the importance of discipline, timing and leadership.

Sun Tzu was born in approximately 544 BCE in the state of Qi in northeastern China. He served as a general and military strategist for the state of Wu in eastern China (which encompassed the modern cities of Shanghai and Nanjing). Living at a time of constant conflict between the fractured states of China, Sun Tzu was well aware of the importance of strategy in warfare and set out his guidance in *The Art of War*. He highlighted the values of swift movement, deception and careful planning at a time when armies were governed by tradition.

Miyamoto Musashi was born in 1584 in Japan and became one of the most celebrated swordsmen of the era. Developing his own school based on the use of two swords, known as *Niten Ichi-ryū*, he fought in more than 60 duels and remained undefeated through his life. Towards the end of his life he composed

The Book of Five Rings, where he provided a guide for budding martial artists. His philosophy emphasised self-mastery, hard work and remaining calm in every situation – values that can be applied to any field.

Inazo Nitobe was born in Japan in 1862, just a few years before the Meiji Restoration upended traditional Japanese society and launched the country into the future. He studied agriculture at university in both Japan and the United States and embarked on a career as both academic and diplomat. He strongly advocated for women's education and served as the first president of the Tokyo Woman's Christian University as well as deputy secretary general of the League of Nations. While devoted to the modernization of Japan, he was also a great defender of traditional Japanese culture and sought to explain its aspects to a wider audience. Writing in English, he published *Bushido: The Soul of Japan* in 1897, an analysis of the samurai and their culture. It was remarkably successful, becoming a bestseller in its time and read by some of the most powerful individuals of the era, including US President Theodore Roosevelt. In this book, he highlighted the virtues at the heart of Japanese culture.

The insights of these books have just as much relevance today as they did when they were originally written. They provide deep insights that can help give advantages in business, sports, politics and everyday life.

The Art of War

Sun Tzu
Translated by Lionel Giles

Contents

Introduction

Sun Tzu's *The Art of War* is probably the earliest-known treatise on war and military science. It is certainly the most influential. Essential reading for strategists in the East since ancient times, it is thought that Napoleon read *The Art of War* when a new edition was published in Paris in 1782.

It was also picked up by two great military theorists who studied Bonaparte's methods – the Prussian Carl von Clausewitz, whose *On War* was published posthumously in 1832, and the French General Baron Antoine-Henri de Jomini, whose *Summary of the Art of War* appeared in 1838.

Also influenced were the pre-Second World War theorists of tank warfare General John Fuller and B.H. Liddell Hart – and, consequently, the German Panzer leaders, including Heinz Guderian, who devoured their work. Field Marshal Bernard Montgomery, victor of El Alamein and commander of land forces on D-Day, wrote extensively on *The Art of War* in his monumental *A History of Warfare*. His great rival, General George Patton, is thought to have read Sun Tzu as a teenager in the Virginia Military Institute before he went to West Point.

General Douglas MacArthur and Joseph Stalin were also said to have been fans of Sun Tzu. *The Art of War* was adopted as a handbook on guerrilla warfare by Mao Zedong, Fidel Castro and Vo Nguyen Giap, the Vietnamese strategist who beat the French and the Americans in Indo-China, and according to

US Marine Corps General Paul K. Van Riper, it influenced the planning of Operation Desert Storm.

The first mention of Sun Tzu as a great military strategist was made, in passing, by the Taoist philosopher Huai-nan Tzu who died in 122BC. The 'Tzu' here, as in the case of Sun Tzu, is an honorific that means 'master'. Sun Tzu – Master Sun – is known more commonly in the literature by his personal name Sun Wu, though 'Wu' might be a nickname as it means 'military'. The surname 'Sun' was said to have been bestowed on Sun Tzu's grandfather by Duke Ching of Ch`i. Ch`i was Sun Tzu's home state which he fled after a rebellion. Sun Tzu would have called himself Ch`ang-ch`ing. This was a so-called 'style', a new name Chinese males of that era adopted at the age of 20.

Sun Tzu fled from Ch`i to the nearby state of Wu where, the great Han historian Ssu-ma Ch'ien (145–85BC) says, *The Art of War* brought him to the attention of Ho Lu, the king of Wu. This must have been before 512BC, as Ssu-ma Ch'ien also records that Sun Tzu was with Ho Lu when Wu attacked the kingdom of Ch'u that year. Ssu-ma Ch'ien also related the story of how Sun Tzu convinced the king of his military prowess.

'I have carefully perused your 13 chapters,' said Ho Lu, king of Wu. 'May I submit your theory of managing soldiers to a slight test?'

Sun Tzu replied: 'You may.'

Ho Lu asked: 'May the test be applied to women?'

The answer again was 'Yes', so arrangements were made to bring 180 ladies out of the palace.

Sun Tzu divided them into two companies, placing one of the king's favourite concubines at the head of each. He then asked them all to take spears in their hands and said: 'I presume you know the difference between front and back, right hand and left hand?'

The women replied: 'Yes.'

'When I say: "Eyes front," you must look straight ahead,' Sun Tzu continued. 'When I say: "Left turn," you must face towards your left hand. When I say: "Right turn," you must face towards your right hand. When I say: "About turn," you must face right round towards your back.'

Having explained the words of command, Sun Tzu began the drill. Then, to the sound of drums, he gave the order, 'Right turn'. But the girls only burst out laughing.

Sun Tzu said: 'If words of command are not clear and distinct, if orders are not thoroughly understood, then the general is to blame.'

So he started drilling them again. This time he gave the order, 'Left turn'. Again the girls burst into fits of laughter. Sun Tzu said again: 'If words of command are not clear and distinct, if orders are not thoroughly understood, the general is to blame. But if his orders are clear, and the soldiers disobey, then it is the fault of their officers.'

So he ordered the leaders of the two companies to be beheaded.

The king of Wu was watching from the top of a raised pavilion. When he saw that his favourite concubines were about to be executed, he quickly sent a message, saying: 'We are now quite satisfied as to our general's ability to handle troops. If we are bereft of these two concubines, our meat and drink will lose their savour. It is our wish that they shall not be beheaded.'

But Sun Tzu replied: 'Having once received His Majesty's commission to be the general of his forces, there are certain commands of His Majesty which, acting in that capacity, I am unable to accept.'

Accordingly, he had the two concubines beheaded and installed another pair as leaders in their place. Then the drum was sounded for the drill again. This time the girls turned right and left, marching ahead or wheeling back, knelt or stood as ordered, all with perfect accuracy and precision, and without venturing a sound.

Then Sun Tzu sent a messenger to the king, saying: 'Your soldiers, Sire, are now properly drilled and disciplined, and ready for Your Majesty's inspection. They can be put to any use that their sovereign may desire; bid them go through fire and water, and they will not disobey...'

After that, Ho Lu saw that Sun Tzu knew how to handle an army, and finally made him a general. In the west, he defeated the Ch`u State and forced his way into Ying, the capital; to the north he put fear into the States of Ch`i and Chin, and spread his fame abroad amongst the feudal princes. And Sun Tzu shared in the might of the king.

In the introduction to his famous 1910 translation of *The Art of War* reprinted here, Lionel Giles cast doubt on this account. He pointed out that the great contemporary chronicle of this period, the Tso Chuan, failed to mention

Sun Tzu among the Wu generals that invaded Ch`u, though lesser figures are mentioned. This has led some to conclude that Sun Tzu did not exist and that *The Art of War* is a compilation of other authors.

From his intimate knowledge of the text, Giles concluded that *The Art of War* was the work of a single author and pointed out that, as a foreigner in Wu, Sun Tzu would not have had the civil rank that was needed to become a general at that time. Clearly, from his writing, the author had practical experience of warfare and had been involved in the attack on Ch`u in 512BC and the capture of Ying in 506BC. However, in the text he mentions conflict with the Yueh. The Wu first attacked the Yueh in 510BC, so *The Art of War* could not have been written before 512BC as Ssu-ma Ch`ien maintained. The Yueh struck back when the Wu were in Ch`u in 505BC. The Wu then counterattacked in 496BC, but were defeated and Ho Lu was killed.

In Chapter VI of *The Art of War*, Sun Tzu writes: 'Though according to my estimate the soldiers of Yueh exceed our own in number, that shall advantage them nothing in the matter of victory. I say then that victory can be achieved.'

This sentence, Giles maintained, was hardly 'one that could have been written in the full flush of victory'. As Ho Lu died in 496BC, if the book was written for him, it must have been written during the period 505–496BC, when there was a lull in the hostilities. Sun Tzu's name does not appear in the historical record again after the death of Ho Lu, but there is no reason to believe that he did not survive to participate in the short-lived resurgence of the Wu who, under Fu Ch`ai, captured the capital of the Yueh in 494BC. The Yueh hit back in 482BC, finally destroying the state of Wu in 473BC. Giles believed that *The Art of War* could also have been written between 496 and 494BC, or 482 and 473BC Ssu-ma Ch`ien's sources might be confused and the drilling of the concubines could have been a preliminary exercise for the work. It is also possible that Ho Lu saw an early draft of the manuscript before 512BC, which was revised later after hostilities with the Yueh broke out.

While Ssu-ma Ch`ien mentioned '13 chapters' and 13 chapters are presented here, some early accounts of *The Art of War* said that there were 82 *p`ien* or chapters. There are several theories about what happened to the other chapters. Giles pointed out that in some shorter works *p`ien* is taken to mean 'leaves'. Sun Tzu's work may have been bound with the work of other military theorists, or various commentaries. It is also thought that the other chapters were records of conversations between Sun Tzu and Ho Lu, discussing the finer points of strategy. One of these appears in the T'ung-tien, an encyclopedic work on government compiled in the 8th century AD by the mandarin Tu Yu. Called '*Nine Configurations and Two Questions*', it appears as a 14th chapter in some editions of *The Art of War*.

Then in 1972 a number of texts engraved on bamboo were found in a grave in Shandong province. Among them were the 13 chapters of Sun Tzu's *Art of War*, though the manuscript was a millennium older than any then known. Alongside were another 33 chapters, but these concerned the practicalities of warfare rather than military strategy and are thought to be the work of a descendant of Sun Tzu's, possibly his grandson, named Sun Pin – 'Sun the Mutilated'. He was said to have been a great general who, according to Ssu-ma Ch`ien, 'had his feet cut off and yet continued to discuss the art of war'. Sun Pin was also reputed to have written a book on warfare that had been lost and the 33 newly discovered chapters are now published as Sun Pin's *The Lost Art of War*.

The 13 chapters presented here are those that have been regarded as the work of the military genius Sun Tzu since antiquity. This is the work that inspired *Napoleon, Mao Zedong et al.* And it is this classic 1910 translation that would have been pored over by Fuller, Liddell Hart, Montgomery and Patton, while

the Allies faced Panzer commanders who had drawn their inspiration from the same source.

In the West, *The Art of War* now has a readership outside military strategists. One of Sun Tzu's great concerns was the politics of war, so it is essential reading for politicians, diplomats and those involved in international relations. Business gurus now teach *The Art of War*, using Sun Tzu's view of warfare as a metaphor for the struggle for global markets. To the Chinese, though, it remains one of the great pillars of classical literature.

For some 2,500 years, Sun Tzu's treatise has had something profound to say about the human condition. The world is no less warlike than it was when the Chinese were slugging it out in the Spring and Autumn (770–476BC) and the Warring States (475–221BC) periods, before the first emperor Shih Huang-ti united China, so undoubtedly Sun Tzu has something to say to us now.

It is also ironic to note that Sun Tzu, perhaps the greatest writer on war, was alive and at work at the same time as China's most illustrious man of peace, the great sage Confucius.

Nigel Cawthorne

Laying Plans

1   Sun Tzu said: The art of war is of vital importance to the State.

2   It is a matter of life and death, a road either to safety or to ruin. Hence it is a subject of inquiry which can on no account be neglected.

3   The art of war, then, is governed by five constant factors, to be taken into account in one's deliberations, when seeking to determine the conditions obtaining in the field.

4   These are:
    (1) The Moral Law;
    (2) Heaven;
    (3) Earth;
    (4) The Commander;
    (5) Method and Discipline.

5 & 6 The Moral Law causes the people to be in complete accord with their ruler, so that they will follow him regardless of their lives, undismayed by any danger.

7   Heaven signifies night and day, cold and heat, times and seasons.

8   Earth comprises distances, great and small; danger and security; open ground and narrow passes; the chances of life and death.

9   The Commander stands for the virtues of wisdom, sincerity, benevolence, courage and strictness.

10 By Method and Discipline are to be understood the marshalling of the army in its proper subdivisions, the graduations of rank among the officers, the maintenance of roads by which supplies may reach the army, and the control of military expenditure.

11 These five heads should be familiar to every general: he who knows them will be victorious; he who knows them not will fail.

12 Therefore, in your deliberations, when seeking to determine the military conditions, let them be made the basis of a comparison, in this wise:—

13 (1) Which of the two sovereigns is imbued with the Moral Law?
    (2) Which of the two generals has most ability?
    (3) With whom lie the advantages derived from Heaven and Earth?
    (4) On which side is Discipline most rigorously enforced?
    (5) Which army is stronger?
    (6) On which side are officers and men more highly trained?
    (7) In which army is there the greater constancy both in reward and
        punishment?

14 By means of these seven considerations I can forecast victory or defeat.

15 The general that hearkens to my counsel and acts upon it, will conquer: let such a one be retained in command! The general that hearkens not to my counsel nor acts upon it, will suffer defeat:— let such a one be dismissed!

16 While heeding the profit of my counsel, avail yourself also of any helpful circumstances over and beyond the ordinary rules.

17 According as circumstances are favourable, one should modify one's plans.

18 All warfare is based on deception.

19 Hence, when able to attack, we must seem unable; when using our forces, we must seem inactive; when we are near, we must make the enemy believe we are far away; when far away, we must make him believe we are near.

20 Hold out baits to entice the enemy. Feign disorder, and crush him.

21 If he is secure at all points, be prepared for him. If he is in superior strength, evade him.

22 If your opponent is of choleric temper, seek to irritate him. Pretend to be weak, that he may grow arrogant.

23 If he is taking his ease, give him no rest. If his forces are united, separate them.

24 Attack him where he is unprepared, appear where you are not expected.

25 These military devices, leading to victory, must not be divulged beforehand.

26 Now the general who wins a battle makes many calculations in his temple ere the battle is fought. The general who loses a battle makes but few calculations beforehand. Thus do many calculations lead to victory, and few calculations to defeat: how much more no calculation at all! It is by attention to this point that I can foresee who is likely to win or lose.

CHAPTER TWO

Waging War

1   Sun Tzu said: In the operations of war, where there are in the field a
thousand swift chariots, as many heavy chariots, and a hundred thousand
mail-clad soldiers, with provisions enough to carry them a thousand li[1], the
expenditure at home and at the front, including entertainment of guests,
small items such as glue and paint, and sums spent on chariots and armour,
will reach the total of a thousand ounces of silver per day. Such is the cost of
raising an army of 100,000 men.

2   When you engage in actual fighting, if victory is long in coming, then men's
weapons will grow dull and their ardour will be damped. If you lay siege to
a town, you will exhaust your strength.

3   Again, if the campaign is protracted, the resources of the State will not be
equal to the strain.

4   Now, when your weapons are dulled, your ardour damped, your strength
exhausted and your treasure spent, other chieftains will spring up to take
advantage of your extremity. Then no man, however wise, will be able to
avert the consequences that must ensue.

---

1   One li is equal to half a kilometre.

5 Thus, though we have heard of stupid haste in war, cleverness has never been seen associated with long delays.

6 There is no instance of a country having benefitted from prolonged warfare.

7 It is only one who is thoroughly acquainted with the evils of war that can thoroughly understand the profitable way of carrying it on.

8 The skilful soldier does not raise a second levy, neither are his supply-wagons loaded more than twice.

9 Bring war material with you from home, but forage on the enemy. Thus the army will have food enough for its needs.

10 Poverty of the State Exchequer causes an army to be maintained by contributions from a distance. Contributing to maintain an army at a distance causes the people to be impoverished.

11 On the other hand, the proximity of an army causes prices to go up; and high prices cause the people's substance to be drained away.

12 When their substance is drained away, the peasantry will be afflicted by heavy exactions.

13&14 With this loss of substance and exhaustion of strength, the homes of the people will be stripped bare, and three-tenths of their income will be dissipated; while government expenses for broken chariots, worn-out horses, breast-plates and helmets, bows and arrows, spears and shields, protective mantles, draught-oxen and heavy wagons, will amount to four-tenths of its total revenue.

15 Hence a wise general makes a point of foraging on the enemy. One cartload of the enemy's provisions is equivalent to twenty of one's own,

and likewise a single *picul*[2] of his provender is equivalent to twenty from one's own store.

16 Now in order to kill the enemy, our men must be roused to anger; that there may be advantage from defeating the enemy, they must have their rewards.

17 Therefore in chariot fighting, when ten or more chariots have been taken, those should be rewarded who took the first. Our own flags should be substituted for those of the enemy, and the chariots mingled and used in conjunction with ours. The captured soldiers should be kindly treated and kept.

18 This is called using the conquered foe to augment one's own strength.

19 In war, then, let your great object be victory, not lengthy campaigns.

20 Thus it may be known that the leader of armies is the arbiter of the people's fate, the man on whom it depends whether the nation shall be in peace or in peril.

---

2 One *picul* weighs approximately 133 lbs.

CHAPTER THREE

Attack by Stratagem

1   Sun Tzu said: In the practical art of war, the best thing of all is to take the enemy's country whole and intact; to shatter and destroy it is not so good. So, too, it is better to recapture an army entire than to destroy it, to capture a regiment, a detachment or a company entire than to destroy them.

2   Hence to fight and conquer in all your battles is not supreme excellence; supreme excellence consists in breaking the enemy's resistance without fighting.

3   Thus the highest form of generalship is to balk the enemy's plans; the next best is to prevent the junction of the enemy's forces; the next in order is to attack the enemy's army in the field; and the worst policy of all is to besiege walled cities.

4   The rule is, not to besiege walled cities if it can possibly be avoided. The preparation of mantlets, movable shelters, and various implements of war, will take up three whole months; and the piling up of mounds against the walls will take three months more.

5   The general, unable to control his irritation, will launch his men to the assault like swarming ants, with the result that one-third of his men are slain, while the town still remains untaken. Such are the disastrous effects of a siege.

6   Therefore the skilful leader subdues the enemy's troops without any fighting; he captures their cities without laying siege to them; he overthrows their kingdom without lengthy operations in the field.

7   With his forces intact he will dispute the mastery of the Empire, and thus, without losing a man, his triumph will be complete. This is the method of attacking by stratagem.

8   It is the rule in war, if our forces are ten to the enemy's one, to surround him; if five to one, to attack him; if twice as numerous, to divide our army into two.

9   If equally matched, we can offer battle; if slightly inferior in numbers, we can avoid the enemy; if quite unequal in every way, we can flee from him.

10   Hence, though an obstinate fight may be made by a small force, in the end it must be captured by the larger force.

11   Now the general is the bulwark of the State; if the bulwark is complete at all points, the State will be strong; if the bulwark is defective, the State will be weak.

12   There are three ways in which a ruler can bring misfortune upon his army:—

13   (1) By commanding the army to advance or to retreat, being ignorant of the fact that it cannot obey. This is called hobbling the army.

14   (2) By attempting to govern an army in the same way as he administers a kingdom, being ignorant of the conditions which obtain in an army. This causes restlessness in the soldier's minds.

15   (3) By employing the officers of his army without discrimination, through ignorance of the military principle of adaptation to circumstances. This shakes the confidence of the soldiers.

16   But when the army is restless and distrustful, trouble is sure to come from the other feudal princes. This is simply bringing anarchy into the army, and flinging victory away.

17 Thus we may know that there are five essentials for victory:

(1) He will win who knows when to fight and when not to fight.
(2) He will win who knows how to handle both superior and inferior forces.
(3) He will win whose army is animated by the same spirit throughout all its ranks.
(4) He will win who, prepared himself, waits to take the enemy unprepared.
(5) He will win who has military capacity and is not interfered with by the sovereign.

18 Hence the saying: If you know the enemy and know yourself, you need not fear the result of a hundred battles. If you know yourself but not the enemy, for every victory gained you will also suffer a defeat. If you know neither the enemy nor yourself, you will succumb in every battle.

CHAPTER FOUR

Tactical Dispositions

1   Sun Tzu said: The good fighters of old first put themselves beyond the possibility of defeat, and then waited for an opportunity of defeating the enemy.

2   To secure ourselves against defeat lies in our own hands, but the opportunity of defeating the enemy is provided by the enemy himself.

3   Thus the good fighter is able to secure himself against defeat, but cannot make certain of defeating the enemy.

4   Hence the saying: One may know how to conquer without being able to do it.

5   Security against defeat implies defensive tactics; ability to defeat the enemy means taking the offensive.

6   Standing on the defensive indicates insufficient strength; attacking, a superabundance of strength.

7   The general who is skilled in defence hides in the most secret recesses of the earth; he who is skilled in attack flashes forth from the topmost heights of heaven. Thus on the one hand we have the ability to protect ourselves; on the other, a victory that is complete.

8   To see victory only when it is within the ken of the common herd is not the acme of excellence.

9   Neither is it the acme of excellence if you fight and conquer and the whole Empire says: 'Well done!'

10 To lift an autumn leaf is no sign of great strength; to see the sun and moon is no sign of sharp sight; to hear the noise of thunder is no sign of a quick ear.

11 What the ancients called a clever fighter is one who not only wins, but excels in winning with ease.

12 Hence his victories bring him neither reputation for wisdom nor credit for courage.

13 He wins his battles by making no mistakes. Making no mistakes is what establishes the certainty of victory, for it means conquering an enemy that is already defeated.

14 Hence the skilful fighter puts himself into a position which makes defeat impossible, and does not miss the moment for defeating the enemy.

15 Thus it is that in war the victorious strategist only seeks battle after the victory has been won, whereas he who is destined to defeat first fights and afterwards looks for victory.

16 The consummate leader cultivates the Moral Law, and strictly adheres to method and discipline; thus it is in his power to control success.

17 In respect of military method, we have, firstly, Measurement; secondly, Estimation of quantity; thirdly, Calculation; fourthly, Balancing of chances; fifthly, Victory.

18 Measurement owes its existence to Earth; Estimation of quantity to Measurement; Calculation to Estimation of quantity; Balancing of chances to Calculation; and Victory to Balancing of chances.

19 A victorious army opposed to a routed one, is as a pound's weight placed in the scale against a single grain.

20 The onrush of a conquering force is like the bursting of pent-up waters into a chasm a thousand fathoms deep.

CHAPTER FIVE

Energy

1   Sun Tzu said: The control of a large force is the same principle as the control of a few men: it is merely a question of dividing up their numbers.

2   Fighting with a large army under your command is nowise different from fighting with a small one: it is merely a question of instituting signs and signals.

3   To ensure that your whole host may withstand the brunt of the enemy's attack and remain unshaken – this is effected by manoeuvres direct and indirect.

4   That the impact of your army may be like a grindstone dashed against an egg – this is effected by the science of weak points and strong.

5   In all fighting, the direct method may be used for joining battle, but indirect methods will be needed in order to secure victory.

6   Indirect tactics, efficiently applied, are inexhaustible as Heaven and Earth, unending as the flow of rivers and streams; like the sun and moon, they end but to begin anew; like the four seasons, they pass away to return once more.

7   There are not more than five musical notes, yet the combinations of these five give rise to more melodies than can ever be heard.

8   There are not more than five primary colours (blue, yellow, red, white and black), yet in combination they produce more hues than can ever be seen.

9   There are not more than five cardinal tastes (sour, acrid, salt, sweet and bitter), yet combinations of them yield more flavours than can ever be tasted.

10 In battle, there are not more than two methods of attack – the direct and the indirect; yet these two in combination give rise to an endless series of manoeuvres.

11 The direct and the indirect lead on to each other in turn. It is like moving in a circle – you never come to an end. Who can exhaust the possibilities of their combination?

12 The onset of troops is like the rush of a torrent which will even roll stones along in its course.

13 The quality of decision is like the well-timed swoop of a falcon which enables it to strike and destroy its victim.

14 Therefore the good fighter will be terrible in his onset, and prompt in his decision.

15 Energy may be likened to the bending of a crossbow; decision, to the releasing of a trigger.

16 Amid the turmoil and tumult of battle, there may be seeming disorder and yet no real disorder at all; amid confusion and chaos, your array may be without head or tail, yet it will be proof against defeat.

17 Simulated disorder postulates perfect discipline, simulated fear postulates courage; simulated weakness postulates strength.

18 Hiding order beneath the cloak of disorder is simply a question of subdivision; concealing courage under a show of timidity presupposes a fund of latent energy; masking strength with weakness is to be effected by tactical dispositions.

19 Thus one who is skilful at keeping the enemy on the move maintains deceitful appearances, according to which the enemy will act. He sacrifices something, that the enemy may snatch at it.

20 By holding out baits, he keeps him on the march; then with a body of picked men he lies in wait for him.

21 The clever combatant looks to the effect of combined energy, and does not require too much from individuals. Hence his ability to pick out the right men and utilize combined energy.

22 When he utilizes combined energy, his fighting men become as it were like unto rolling logs or stones. For it is the nature of a log or stone to remain motionless on level ground, and to move when on a slope; if four-cornered, to come to a standstill, but if round-shaped, to go rolling down.

23 Thus the energy developed by good fighting men is as the momentum of a round stone rolled down a mountain thousands of feet in height. So much on the subject of energy.

CHAPTER SIX

Weak Points and Strong

1   Sun Tzu said: Whoever is first in the field and awaits the coming of the enemy, will be fresh for the fight; whoever is second in the field and has to hasten to battle will arrive exhausted.

2   Therefore the clever combatant imposes his will on the enemy, but does not allow the enemy's will to be imposed on him.

3   By holding out advantages to him, he can cause the enemy to approach of his own accord; or, by inflicting damage, he can make it impossible for the enemy to draw near.

4   If the enemy is taking his ease, he can harass him; if well supplied with food, he can starve him out; if quietly encamped, he can force him to move.

5   Appear at points which the enemy must hasten to defend; march swiftly to places where you are not expected.

6   An army may march great distances without distress, if it marches through country where the enemy is not.

7   You can be sure of succeeding in your attacks if you only attack places which are undefended. You can ensure the safety of your defence if you only hold positions that cannot be attacked.

8   Hence that general is skilful in attack whose opponent does not know what to defend; and he is skilful in defence whose opponent does not know what to attack.

9   O divine art of subtlety and secrecy! Through you we learn to be invisible, through you inaudible; and hence we can hold the enemy's fate in our hands.

10 You may advance and be absolutely irresistible, if you make for the enemy's weak points; you may retire and be safe from pursuit if your movements are more rapid than those of the enemy.

11 If we wish to fight, the enemy can be forced to an engagement even though he be sheltered behind a high rampart and a deep ditch. All we need do is attack some other place that he will be obliged to relieve.

12 If we do not wish to fight, we can prevent the enemy from engaging us even though the lines of our encampment be merely traced out on the ground. All we need do is to throw something odd and unaccountable in his way.

13 By discovering the enemy's dispositions and remaining invisible ourselves, we can keep our forces concentrated, while the enemy's must be divided.

14 We can form a single united body, while the enemy must split up into fractions. Hence there will be a whole pitted against separate parts of a whole, which means that we shall be many to the enemy's few.

15 And if we are able thus to attack an inferior force with a superior one, our opponents will be in dire straits.

16 The spot where we intend to fight must not be made known; for then the enemy will have to prepare against a possible attack at several different points; and his forces being thus distributed in many directions, the numbers we shall have to face at any given point will be proportionately few.

17 For should the enemy strengthen his van, he will weaken his rear; should he strengthen his rear, he will weaken his van; should he strengthen his left, he will weaken his right; should he strengthen his right, he will weaken his left. If he sends reinforcements everywhere, he will everywhere be weak.

18 Numerical weakness comes from having to prepare against possible attacks; numerical strength, from compelling our adversary to make these preparations against us.

19 Knowing the place and the time of the coming battle, we may concentrate from the greatest distances in order to fight.

20 But if neither time nor place be known, then the left wing will be impotent to succour the right, the right equally impotent to succour the left, the van unable to relieve the rear, or the rear to support the van. How much more so if the furthest portions of the army are anything under a hundred *li* apart, and even the nearest are separated by several *li*!

21 Though according to my estimate the soldiers of Yueh exceed our own in number, that shall advantage them nothing in the matter of victory. I say then that victory can be achieved.

22 Though the enemy be stronger in numbers, we may prevent him from fighting. Scheme so as to discover his plans and the likelihood of their success.

23 Rouse him, and learn the principle of his activity or inactivity. Force him to reveal himself, so as to find out his vulnerable spots.

24 Carefully compare the opposing army with your own, so that you may know where strength is superabundant and where it is deficient.

25 In making tactical dispositions, the highest pitch you can attain is to conceal them; conceal your dispositions, and you will be safe from the prying of the subtlest spies, from the machinations of the wisest brains.

26 How victory may be produced for them out of the enemy's own tactics – that is what the multitude cannot comprehend.

27 All men can see the tactics whereby I conquer, but what none can see is the strategy out of which victory is evolved.

28 Do not repeat the tactics which have gained you one victory, but let your methods be regulated by the infinite variety of circumstances.

29 Military tactics are like unto water; for water in its natural course runs away from high places and hastens downwards.

30 So in war, the way is to avoid what is strong and to strike at what is weak.

31 Water shapes its course according to the nature of the ground over which it flows; the soldier works out his victory in relation to the foe whom he is facing.

32 Therefore, just as water retains no constant shape, so in warfare there are no constant conditions.

33 He who can modify his tactics in relation to his opponent and thereby succeed in winning, may be called a heaven-born captain.

34 The five elements (water, fire, wood, metal, earth) are not always equally predominant; the four seasons make way for each other in turn. There are short days and long; the moon has its periods of waning and waxing.

CHAPTER SEVEN

Manoeuvring

1   Sun Tzu said: In war, the general receives his commands from the sovereign.

2   Having collected an army and concentrated his forces, he must blend and harmonize the different elements thereof before pitching his camp.

3   After that, comes tactical manoeuvring, than which there is nothing more difficult. The difficulty of tactical manoeuvring consists in turning the devious into the direct, and misfortune into gain.

4   Thus, to take a long and circuitous route, after enticing the enemy out of the way, and though starting after him, to contrive to reach the goal before him, shows knowledge of the artifice of deviation.

5   Manoeuvring with an army is advantageous; with an undisciplined multitude, most dangerous.

6   If you set a fully equipped army in march in order to snatch an advantage, the chances are that you will be too late. On the other hand, to detach a flying column for the purpose involves the sacrifice of its baggage and stores.

7 Thus, if you order your men to roll up their buff-coats, and make forced marches without halting day or night, covering double the usual distance at a stretch, doing a hundred *li* in order to wrest an advantage, the leaders of all your three divisions will fall into the hands of the enemy.

8 The stronger men will be in front, the jaded ones will fall behind, and on this plan only one-tenth of your army will reach its destination.

9 If you march fifty *li* in order to outmanoeuvre the enemy, you will lose the leader of your first division, and only half your force will reach the goal.

10 If you march thirty *li* with the same object, two-thirds of your army will arrive.

11 We may take it then that an army without its baggage-train is lost; without provisions it is lost; without bases of supply it is lost.

12 We cannot enter into alliances until we are acquainted with the designs of our neighbours.

13 We are not fit to lead an army on the march unless we are familiar with the face of the country – its mountains and forests, its pitfalls and precipices, its marshes and swamps.

14 We shall be unable to turn natural advantage to account unless we make use of local guides.

15 In war, practise dissimulation, and you will succeed.

16 Whether to concentrate or to divide your troops must be decided by circumstances.

17 Let your rapidity be that of the wind, your compactness be that of the forest.

18 In raiding and plundering be like fire, in immovability like a mountain.

19 Let your plans be dark and impenetrable as night, and when you move, fall like a thunderbolt.

20 When you plunder a countryside, let the spoil be divided amongst your men; when you capture new territory, cut it up into allotments for the benefit of the soldiery.

21 Ponder and deliberate before you make a move.

22 He will conquer who has learnt the artifice of deviation. Such is the art of manoeuvring.

23 The Book of Army Management says: On the field of battle, the spoken word does not carry far enough: hence the institution of gongs and drums. Nor can ordinary objects be seen clearly enough: hence the institution of banners and flags.

24 Gongs and drums, banners and flags, are means whereby the ears and eyes of the host may be focused on one particular point.

25 The host thus forming a single united body, it is impossible either for the brave to advance alone, or for the cowardly to retreat alone. This is the art of handling large masses of men.

26 In night-fighting, then, make much use of signal-fires and drums, and in fighting by day, of flags and banners, as a means of influencing the ears and eyes of your army.

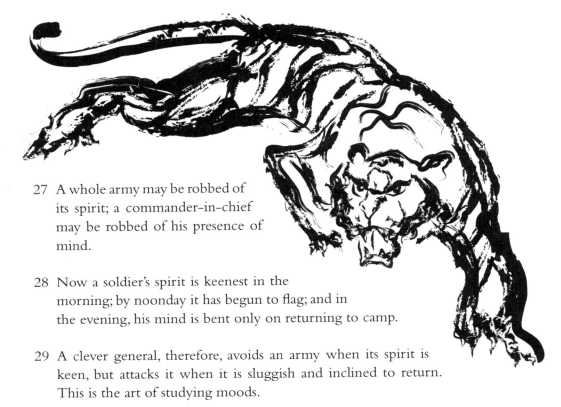

27 A whole army may be robbed of
its spirit; a commander-in-chief
may be robbed of his presence of
mind.

28 Now a soldier's spirit is keenest in the
morning; by noonday it has begun to flag; and in
the evening, his mind is bent only on returning to camp.

29 A clever general, therefore, avoids an army when its spirit is
keen, but attacks it when it is sluggish and inclined to return.
This is the art of studying moods.

30 Disciplined and calm, to await the appearance of disorder and hubbub
amongst the enemy: – this is the art of retaining self-possession.

31 To be near the goal while the enemy is still far from it, to wait at ease
while the enemy is toiling and struggling, to be well-fed while the enemy is
famished: – this is the art of husbanding one's strength.

32 To refrain from intercepting an enemy whose banners are in perfect order,
to refrain from attacking an army drawn up in calm and confident array: –
this is the art of studying circumstances.

33 It is a military axiom not to advance uphill against the enemy, nor to oppose him when he comes downhill.

34 Do not pursue an enemy who simulates flight; do not attack soldiers whose temper is keen.

35 Do not swallow bait offered by the enemy. Do not interfere with an army that is returning home.

36 When you surround an army, leave an outlet free. Do not press a desperate foe too hard.

37 Such is the art of warfare.

CHAPTER EIGHT

Variation in Tactics

1 Sun Tzu said: In war, the general receives his commands from the sovereign, collects his army and concentrates his forces.

2 When in difficult country, do not encamp. In country where high roads intersect, join hands with your allies. Do not linger in dangerously isolated positions. In hemmed-in situations, you must resort to stratagem. In desperate positions, you must fight.

3 There are roads which must not be followed, armies which must not be attacked, towns which must not be besieged, positions which must not be contested, commands of the sovereign which must not be obeyed.

4 The general who thoroughly understands the advantages that accompany variation of tactics knows how to handle his troops.

5 The general who does not understand these, may be well acquainted with the configuration of the country, yet he will not be able to turn his knowledge to practical account.

6   So, the student of war who is unversed in the art of war of varying his plans, even though he be acquainted with the Five Advantages, will fail to make the best use of his men.

7   Hence in the wise leader's plans, considerations of advantage and of disadvantage will be blended together.

8   If our expectation of advantage be tempered in this way, we may succeed in accomplishing the essential part of our schemes.

9   If, on the other hand, in the midst of difficulties we are always ready to seize an advantage, we may extricate ourselves from misfortune.

10 Reduce the hostile chiefs by inflicting damage on them; and make trouble for them, and keep them constantly engaged; hold out specious allurements, and make them rush to any given point.

11 The art of war teaches us to rely not on the likelihood of the enemy's not coming, but on our own readiness to receive him; not on the chance of his not attacking, but rather on the fact that we have made our position unassailable.

12 There are five dangerous faults which may affect a general:

(1) Recklessness, which leads to destruction;
(2) cowardice, which leads to capture;
(3) a hasty temper, which can be provoked by insults;
(4) a delicacy of honour which is sensitive to shame;
(5) over-solicitude for his men, which exposes him to worry and trouble.

13 These are the five besetting sins of a general, ruinous to the conduct of war.

14 When an army is overthrown and its leader slain, the cause will surely be found among these five dangerous faults. Let them be a subject of meditation.

CHAPTER NINE

The Army on the March

1   Sun Tzu said: We come now to the question of encamping the army, and observing signs of the enemy. Pass quickly over mountains, and keep in the neighbourhood of valleys.

2   Camp in high places, facing the sun. Do not climb heights in order to fight. So much for mountain warfare.

3   After crossing a river, you should get far away from it.

4   When an invading force crosses a river in its onward march, do not advance to meet it in mid-stream. It will be best to let half the army get across, and then deliver your attack.

5   If you are anxious to fight, you should not go to meet the invader near a river which he has to cross.

6   Moor your craft higher up than the enemy, and facing the sun. Do not move up-stream to meet the enemy. So much for river warfare.

7 In crossing salt-marshes, your sole concern should be to get over them quickly, without any delay.

8 If forced to fight in a salt-marsh, you should have water and grass near you, and get your back to a clump of trees. So much for operations in salt-marshes.

9 In dry, level country, take up an easily accessible position with rising ground to your right and on your rear, so that the danger may be in front, and safety lie behind. So much for campaigning in flat country.

10 These are the four useful branches of military knowledge which enabled the Yellow Emperor to vanquish four other sovereigns.

11 All armies prefer high ground to low and sunny places to dark.

12 If you are careful of your men, and camp on hard ground, the army will be free from disease of every kind, and this will spell victory.

13 When you come to a hill or a bank, occupy the sunny side, with the slope on your right rear. Thus you will at once act for the benefit of your soldiers and utilize the natural advantages of the ground.

14 When, in consequence of heavy rains up-country, a river which you wish to ford is swollen and flecked with foam, you must wait until it subsides.

15 Country in which there are precipitous cliffs with torrents running between, deep natural hollows, confined places, tangled thickets, quagmires and crevasses, should be left with all possible speed and not approached.

16 While we keep away from such places, we should get the enemy to approach them; while we face them, we should let the enemy have them on his rear.

17 If in the neighbourhood of your camp there should be any hilly country, ponds surrounded by aquatic grass, hollow basins filled with reeds, or woods with thick undergrowth, they must be carefully routed out and searched; for these are places where men in ambush or insidious spies are likely to be lurking.

18 When the enemy is close at hand and remains quiet, he is relying on the natural strength of his position.

19 When he keeps aloof and tries to provoke a battle, he is anxious for the other side to advance.

20 If his place of encampment is easy of access, he is tendering a bait.

21 Movement amongst the trees of a forest shows that the enemy is advancing. The appearance of a number of screens in the midst of thick grass means that the enemy wants to make us suspicious.

22 The rising of birds in their flight is the sign of an ambuscade. Startled beasts indicate that a sudden attack is coming.

23 When there is dust rising in a high column, it is the sign of chariots advancing; when the dust is low, but spread over a wide area, it betokens the approach of infantry. When it branches out in different directions, it shows that parties have been sent to collect firewood. A few clouds of dust moving to and fro signify that the army is encamping.

24 Humble words and increased preparations are signs that the enemy is about to advance. Violent language and driving forward as if to the attack are signs that he will retreat.

25 When the light chariots come out first and take up a position on the wings, it is a sign that the enemy is forming for battle.

26 Peace proposals unaccompanied by a sworn covenant indicate a plot.

27 When there is much running about and the soldiers fall into rank, it means that the critical moment has come.

28 When some are seen advancing and some retreating, it is a lure.

29 When the soldiers stand leaning on their spears, they are faint from want of food.

30 If those who are sent to draw water begin by drinking themselves, the army is suffering from thirst.

31 If the enemy sees an advantage to be gained and makes no effort to secure it, the soldiers are exhausted.

32 If birds gather on any spot, it is unoccupied. Clamour by night betokens nervousness.

33 If there is disturbance in the camp, the general's authority is weak. If the banners and flags are shifted about, sedition is afoot. If the officers are angry, it means that the men are weary.

34 When an army feeds its horses with grain and kills its cattle for food, and when the men do not hang their cooking-pots over the camp-fires, showing that they will not return to their tents, you may know that they are determined to fight to the death.

35 The sight of men whispering together in small knots or speaking in subdued tones points to disaffection amongst the rank and file.

36 Too frequent rewards signify that the enemy is at the end of his resources; too many punishments betray a condition of dire distress.

37 To begin by bluster, but afterwards to take fright at the enemy's numbers, shows a supreme lack of intelligence.

38 When envoys are sent with compliments in their mouths, it is a sign that the enemy wishes for a truce.

39 If the enemy's troops march up angrily and remain facing ours for a long time without either joining battle or taking themselves off again, the situation is one that demands great vigilance and circumspection.

40 If our troops are no more in number than the enemy, that is amply sufficient; it only means that no direct attack can be made. What we can do is simply to concentrate all our available strength, keep a close watch on the enemy, and obtain reinforcements.

41 He who exercises no forethought but makes light of his opponents is sure to be captured by them.

42 If soldiers are punished before they have grown attached to you, they will not prove submissive; and, unless submissive, they will be practically useless. If, when the soldiers have become attached to you, punishments are not enforced, they will still be useless.

43 Therefore soldiers must be treated in the first instance with humanity, but kept under control by means of iron discipline. This is a certain road to victory.

44 If in training soldiers commands are habitually enforced, the army will be well-disciplined; if not, its discipline will be bad.

45 If a general shows confidence in his men but always insists on his orders being obeyed, the gain will be mutual.

CHAPTER TEN

Terrain

1   Sun Tzu said: We may distinguish six kinds of terrain, to wit:

(1) Accessible ground;
(2) entangling ground;
(3) temporizing ground;
(4) narrow passes;
(5) precipitous heights;
(6) positions at a great distance from the enemy.

2   Ground which can be freely traversed by both sides is called accessible.

3   With regard to ground of this nature, be before the enemy in occupying the raised and sunny spots, and carefully guard your line of supplies. Then you will be able to fight with advantage.

4   Ground which can be abandoned but is hard to re-occupy is called entangling.

5   From a position of this sort, if the enemy is unprepared, you may sally forth and defeat him. But if the enemy is prepared for your coming, and you fail to defeat him, then, return being impossible, disaster will ensue.

6   When the position is such that neither side will gain by making the first move, it is called temporizing ground.

7   In a position of this sort, even though the enemy should offer us an attractive bait, it will be advisable not to stir forth, but rather to retreat, thus enticing the enemy in his turn; then, when part of his army has come out, we may deliver our attack with advantage.

8   With regard to narrow passes, if you can occupy them first, let them be strongly garrisoned and await the advent of the enemy.

9   Should the army forestall you in occupying a pass, do not go after him if the pass is fully garrisoned, but only if it is weakly garrisoned.

10 With regard to precipitous heights, if you are beforehand with your adversary, you should occupy the raised and sunny spots, and there wait for him to come up.

11 If the enemy has occupied them before you, do not follow him, but retreat and try to entice him away.

12 If you are situated at a great distance from the enemy, and the strength of the two armies is equal, it is not easy to provoke a battle, and fighting will be to your disadvantage.

13 These six are the principles connected with Earth. The general who has attained a responsible post must be careful to study them.

14 Now an army is exposed to six calamities, not arising from natural causes, but from faults for which the general is responsible. These are:

(1) Flight;
(2) insubordination;

(3) collapse;
(4) ruin;
(5) disorganization;
(6) rout.

15 Other conditions being equal, if one force is hurled against another ten times its size, the result will be the flight of the former.

16 When the common soldiers are too strong and their officers too weak, the result is insubordination. When the officers are too strong and the common soldiers too weak, the result is collapse.

17 When the higher officers are angry and insubordinate, and on meeting the enemy give battle on their own account from a feeling of resentment, before the commander-in-chief can tell whether or not he is in a position to fight, the result is ruin.

18 When the general is weak and without authority; when his orders are not clear and distinct; when there are no fixed duties assigned to officers and men, and the ranks are formed in a slovenly haphazard manner, the result is utter disorganization.

19 When a general, unable to estimate the enemy's strength, allows an inferior force to engage a larger one, or hurls a weak detachment against a powerful one, and neglects to place picked soldiers in the front rank, the result must be a rout.

20 These are six ways of courting defeat, which must be carefully noted by the general who has attained a responsible post.

21 The natural formation of the country is the soldier's best ally; but a power of estimating the adversary, of controlling the forces of victory, and of shrewdly calculating difficulties, dangers and distances, constitutes the test of a great general.

22 He who knows these things, and in fighting puts his knowledge into practice, will win his battles. He who knows them not, nor practises them, will surely be defeated.

23 If fighting is sure to result in victory, then you must fight, even though the ruler forbid it; if fighting will not result in victory, then you must not fight even at the ruler's bidding.

24 The general who advances without coveting fame and retreats without fearing disgrace, whose only thought is to protect his country and do good service for his sovereign, is the jewel of the kingdom.

25 Regard your soldiers as your children, and they will follow you into the deepest valleys; look upon them as your own beloved sons, and they will stand by you even unto death.

26 If, however, you are indulgent, but unable to make your authority felt; kind-hearted, but unable to enforce your commands; and incapable, moreover, of quelling disorder: then your soldiers must be likened to spoilt children; they are useless for any practical purpose.

27 If we know that our own men are in a condition to attack, but are unaware that the enemy is not open to attack, we have gone only halfway towards victory.

28 If we know that the enemy is open to attack, but are unaware that our own men are not in a condition to attack, we have gone only halfway towards victory.

29 If we know that the enemy is open to attack, and also know our men are in a condition to attack, but are unaware that the nature of the ground makes fighting impracticable, we have still gone only halfway towards victory.

30 Hence the experienced soldier, once in motion, is never bewildered; once he has broken camp, he is never at a loss.

31 Hence the saying: If you know the enemy and know yourself, your victory will not stand in doubt; if you know Heaven and know Earth, you may make your victory complete.

CHAPTER ELEVEN

The Nine Situations

1 Sun Tzu said: The art of war recognizes nine varieties of ground:

(1) Dispersive ground;
(2) facile ground;
(3) contentious ground;
(4) open ground;
(5) ground of intersecting highways;
(6) serious ground;
(7) difficult ground;
(8) hemmed–in ground;
(9) desperate ground.

2 When a chieftain is fighting in his own territory, it is dispersive ground.

3 When he has penetrated into hostile territory, but to no great distance, it is facile ground.

4 Ground the possession of which imports great advantage to either side, is contentious ground.

5 Ground on which each side has liberty of movement is open ground.

6   Ground which forms the key to three contiguous states, so that he who occupies it first has most of the Empire at his command, is a ground of intersecting highways.

7   When an army has penetrated into the heart of a hostile country, leaving a number of fortified cities in its rear, it is serious ground.

8   Mountain forests, rugged steeps, marshes and fens – all country that is hard to traverse: this is difficult ground.

9   Ground which is reached through narrow gorges, and from which we can only retire by tortuous paths, so that a small number of the enemy would suffice to crush a large body of our men: this is hemmed-in ground.

10   Ground on which we can only be saved from destruction by fighting without delay, is desperate ground.

11   On dispersive ground, therefore, fight not. On facile ground, halt not. On contentious ground, attack not.

12   On open ground, do not try to block the enemy's way. On the ground of intersecting highways, join hands with your allies.

13   On serious ground, gather in plunder. In difficult ground, keep steadily on the march.

14   On hemmed-in ground, resort to stratagem. On desperate ground, fight.

15   Those who were called skilful leaders of old knew how to drive a wedge between the enemy's front and rear; to prevent co-operation between his large and small divisions; to hinder the good troops from rescuing the bad, the officers from rallying their men.

16 When the enemy's men were united, they managed to keep them in disorder.

17 When it was to their advantage, they made a forward move; when otherwise, they stopped still.

18 If asked how to cope with a great host of the enemy in orderly array and on the point of marching to the attack, I should say: 'Begin by seizing something which your opponent holds dear; then he will be amenable to your will.'

19 Rapidity is the essence of war: take advantage of the enemy's unreadiness, make your way by unexpected routes, and attack unguarded spots.

20 The following are the principles to be observed by an invading force: The further you penetrate into a country, the greater will be the solidarity of your troops, and thus the defenders will not prevail against you.

21 Make forays in fertile country in order to supply your army with food.

22 Carefully study the well-being of your men, and do not overtax them. Concentrate your energy and hoard your strength. Keep your army continually on the move, and devise unfathomable plans.

23 Throw your soldiers into positions whence there is no escape, and they will prefer death to flight. If they will face death, there is nothing they may not achieve. Officers and men alike will put forth their uttermost strength.

24 Soldiers when in desperate straits lose the sense of fear. If there is no place of refuge, they will stand firm. If they are in hostile country, they will show a stubborn front. If there is no help for it, they will fight hard.

25 Thus, without waiting to be marshalled, the soldiers will be constantly on the qui vive; without waiting to be asked, they will do your will; without restrictions, they will be faithful; without giving orders, they can be trusted.

26 Prohibit the taking of omens, and do away with superstitious doubts. Then, until death itself comes, no calamity need be feared.

27 If our soldiers are not overburdened with money, it is not because they have a distaste for riches; if their lives are not unduly long, it is not because they are disinclined to longevity.

28 On the day they are ordered out to battle, your soldiers may weep, those sitting up bedewing their garments, and those lying down letting the tears run down their cheeks. But let them once be brought to bay, and they will display the courage of a Chu or a Kuei.

29 The skilful tactician may be likened to the shuai-jan. Now the shuai-jan is a snake that is found in the Ch'ang mountains. Strike at its head, and you will be attacked by its tail; strike at its tail, and you will be attacked by its head; strike at its middle, and you will be attacked by head and tail both.

30 Asked if an army can be made to imitate the shuai-jan, I should answer, 'Yes'. For the men of Wu and the men of Yueh are enemies; yet if they are crossing a river in the same boat and are caught by a storm, they will come to each other's assistance just as the left hand helps the right.

31 Hence it is not enough to put one's trust in the tethering of horses, and the burying of chariot wheels in the ground.

32 The principle on which to manage an army is to set up one standard of courage which all must reach.

33 How to make the best of both strong and weak, that is a question involving the proper use of ground.

34 Thus the skilful general conducts his army just as though he were leading a single man, willy-nilly, by the hand.

35 It is the business of a general to be quiet and thus ensure secrecy; upright and just, and thus maintain order.

36 He must be able to mystify his officers and men by false reports and appearances, and thus keep them in total ignorance.

37 By altering his arrangements and changing his plans, he keeps the enemy without definite knowledge. By shifting his camp and taking circuitous routes, he prevents the enemy from anticipating his purpose.

38 At the critical moment, the leader of an army acts like one who has climbed up a height and then kicks away the ladder behind him. He carries his men deep into hostile territory before he shows his hand.

39 He burns his boats and breaks his cooking-pots; like a shepherd driving a flock of sheep, he drives his men this way and that, and nothing knows whither he is going.

40 To muster his host and bring it into danger: – this may be termed the business of the general.

41 The different measures suited to the nine varieties of ground; the expediency of aggressive or defensive tactics; and the fundamental laws of human nature: these are things that must most certainly be studied.

42 When invading hostile territory, the general principle is that penetrating deeply brings cohesion; penetrating but a short way means dispersion.

43 When you leave your own country behind, and take your army across neighbourhood territory, you find yourself on critical ground. When there are means of communication on all four sides, the ground is one of intersecting highways.

44 When you penetrate deeply into a country, it is serious ground. When you penetrate but a little way, it is facile ground.

45 When you have the enemy's strongholds in your rear, and narrow passes in front, it is hemmed-in ground. When there is no place of refuge at all, it is desperate ground.

46 Therefore, on dispersive ground, I would inspire my men with unity of purpose. On facile ground, I would see that there is close connection between all parts of my army.

47 On contentious ground, I would hurry up my rear.

48 On open ground, I would keep a vigilant eye on my defences. On ground of intersecting highways, I would consolidate my alliances.

49 On serious ground, I would try to ensure a continuous stream of supplies. On difficult ground, I would keep pushing on along the road.

50 On hemmed-in ground, I would block any way of retreat. On desperate ground, I would proclaim to my soldiers the hopelessness of saving their lives.

51 For it is the soldier's disposition to offer an obstinate resistance when surrounded, to fight hard when he cannot help himself, and to obey promptly when he has fallen into danger.

52 We cannot enter into alliance with neighbouring princes until we are acquainted with their designs. We are not fit to lead an army on the march unless we are familiar with the face of the country – its mountains and forests, its pitfalls and precipices, its marshes and swamps. We shall be unable to turn natural advantages to account unless we make use of local guides.

53 To be ignorant of any one of the following four or five principles does not befit a warlike prince.

54 When a warlike prince attacks a powerful state, his generalship shows itself in preventing the concentration of the enemy's forces. He overawes his opponents, and their allies are prevented from joining against him.

55 Hence he does not strive to ally himself with all and sundry, nor does he foster the power of other states. He carries out his own secret designs, keeping his antagonists in awe. Thus he is able to capture their cities and overthrow their kingdoms.

56 Bestow rewards without regard to rule, issue orders without regard to previous arrangements; and you will be able to handle a whole army as though you had to do with but a single man.

57 Confront your soldiers with the deed itself; never let them know your design. When the outlook is bright, bring it before their eyes; but tell them nothing when the situation is gloomy.

58 Place your army in deadly peril, and it will survive; plunge it into desperate straits, and it will come off in safety.

59 For it is precisely when a force has fallen into harm's way that it is capable of striking a blow for victory.

60 Success in warfare is gained by carefully accommodating ourselves to the enemy's purpose.

61 By persistently hanging on the enemy's flank, we shall succeed in the long run in killing the commander-in-chief.

62 This is called the ability to accomplish a thing by sheer cunning.

63 On the day that you take up your command, block the frontier passes, destroy the official tallies, and stop the passage of all emissaries.

64 Be stern in the council-chamber, so that you may control the situation.

65 If the enemy leaves a door open, you must rush in.

66 Forestall your opponent by seizing what he holds dear, and subtly contrive to time his arrival on the ground.

67 Walk in the path defined by rule, and accommodate yourself to the enemy until you can fight a decisive battle.

68 At first, then, exhibit the coyness of a maiden, until the enemy gives you an opening; afterwards emulate the rapidity of a running hare, and it will be too late for the enemy to oppose you.

CHAPTER TWELVE

Attack by Fire

1   Sun Tzu said: There are five ways of attacking with fire. The first is to burn soldiers in their camp; the second is to burn stores; the third is to burn baggage trains; the fourth is to burn arsenals and magazines; the fifth is to hurl dropping fire amongst the enemy.

2   In order to carry out an attack, we must have means available. The material for raising fire should always be kept in readiness.

3   There is a proper season for making attacks with fire, and special days for starting a conflagration.

4   The proper season is when the weather is very dry; the special days are those when the moon is in the constellations of the Sieve, the Wall, the Wing or the Cross-bar; for these four are all days of rising wind.

5   In attacking with fire, one should be prepared to meet five possible developments:

6   (1) When fire breaks out inside the enemy's camp, respond at once with an attack from without.

7   (2) If there is an outbreak of fire, but the enemy's soldiers remain quiet, bide your time and do not attack.

8   (3) When the force of the flames has reached its height, follow it up with an attack, if that is practicable; if not, stay where you are.

9   (4) If it is possible to make an assault with fire from without, do not wait for it to break out within, but deliver your attack at a favourable moment.

10   (5) When you start a fire, be to windward of it. Do not attack from the leeward.

11   A wind that rises in the daytime lasts long, but a night breeze soon falls.

12   In every army, the five developments connected with fire must be known, the movements of the stars calculated, and a watch kept for the proper days.

13   Hence those who use fire as an aid to the attack show intelligence; those who use water as an aid to the attack gain an accession of strength.

14   By means of water, an enemy may be intercepted, but not robbed of all his belongings.

15   Unhappy is the fate of one who tries to win his battles and succeed in his attacks without cultivating the spirit of enterprise; for the result is waste of time and general stagnation.

16   Hence the saying: The enlightened ruler lays his plans well ahead; the good general cultivates his resources.

17   Move not unless you see an advantage; use not your troops unless there is something to be gained; fight not unless the position is critical.

18 No ruler should put troops into the field merely to gratify his own spleen; no general should fight a battle simply out of pique.

19 If it is to your advantage, make a forward move; if not, stay where you are.

20 Anger may in time change to gladness; vexation may be succeeded by content.

21 But a kingdom that has once been destroyed can never come again into being; nor can the dead ever be brought back to life.

22 Hence the enlightened ruler is heedful, and the good general full of caution. This is the way to keep a country at peace and an army intact.

The Use of Spies

1   Sun Tzu said: Raising a host of a hundred thousand men and marching them great distances entails heavy loss on the people and a drain on the resources of the State. The daily expenditure will amount to a thousand ounces of silver. There will be commotion at home and abroad, and men will drop down exhausted on the highways. As many as seven hundred thousand families will be impeded in their labour.

2   Hostile armies may face each other for years, striving for the victory which is decided in a single day. This being so, to remain in ignorance of the enemy's condition simply because one grudges the outlay of a hundred ounces of silver in honours and emoluments, is the height of inhumanity.

3   One who acts thus is no leader of men, no present help to his sovereign, no master of victory.

4   Thus, what enables the wise sovereign and the good general to strike and conquer, and achieve things beyond the reach of ordinary men, is foreknowledge.

5   Now this foreknowledge cannot be elicited from spirits; it cannot be obtained inductively from experience, nor by any deductive calculation.

6   Knowledge of the enemy's dispositions can only be obtained from other men.

7   Hence the use of spies, of whom there are five classes:
    (1) Local spies;
    (2) inward spies;
    (3) converted spies;
    (4) doomed spies;
    (5) surviving spies.

8   When these five kinds of spy are all at work, none can discover the secret system. This is called 'divine manipulation of the threads'. It is the sovereign's most precious faculty.

9   Having local spies means employing the services of the inhabitants of a district.

10 Having inward spies, means making use of officials of the enemy.

11 Having converted spies, means getting hold of the enemy's spies and using them for our own purposes.

12 Having doomed spies, doing certain things openly for purposes of deception, and allowing our spies to know of them and report them to the enemy.

13 Surviving spies, finally, are those who bring back news from the enemy's camp.

14 Hence it is that with none in the whole army are more intimate relations to be maintained than with spies. None should be more liberally rewarded. In no other business should greater secrecy be preserved.

15 Spies cannot be usefully employed without a certain intuitive sagacity.

16 They cannot be properly managed without benevolence and straight-forwardness.

17 Without subtle ingenuity of mind, one cannot make certain of the truth of their reports.

18 Be subtle! be subtle! and use your spies for every kind of business.

19 If a secret piece of news is divulged by a spy before the time is ripe, he must be put to death together with the man to whom the secret was told.

20 Whether the object be to crush an army, to storm a city, or to assassinate an individual, it is always necessary to begin by finding out the names of the attendants, the aides-de-camp, and door-keepers and sentries of the general in command. Our spies must be commissioned to ascertain these.

21 The enemy's spies who have come to spy on us must be sought out, tempted with bribes, led away and comfortably housed. Thus they will become converted spies and available for our service.

22 It is through the information brought by the converted spy that we are able to acquire and employ local and inward spies.

23 It is owing to his information, again, that we can cause the doomed spy to carry false tidings to the enemy.

24 Lastly, it is by his information that the surviving spy can be used on appointed occasions.

25 The end and aim of spying in all its five varieties is knowledge of the enemy; and this knowledge can only be derived, in the first instance, from the converted spy. Hence it is essential that the converted spy be treated with the utmost liberality.

26 Of old, the rise of the Yin dynasty was due to I Chih who had served under the Hsia. Likewise, the rise of the Chou dynasty was due to Lu Ya who had served under the Yin.

27 Hence it is only the enlightened ruler and the wise general who will use the highest intelligence of the army for purposes of spying and thereby they achieve great results. Spies are a most important element in warfare, because on them depends an army's ability

The Book of Five Rings

Miyamoto Musashi
Translated by Victor Harris

Contents

Introduction

Japan during Musashi's lifetime

Miyamoto Musashi was born in 1584, in a Japan struggling to recover from more than four centuries of internal strife. The traditional rule of the emperors had been overthrown in the twelfth century, and although each successive emperor remained the figurehead of Japan, his powers were very much reduced. Since that time, Japan had seen almost continuous civil war between the provincial lords, warrior monks and brigands, all fighting one another for land and power. In the fifteenth and sixteenth centuries the lords, called *daimyō*, built huge stone castles to protect themselves and their lands, and castle towns outside the walls began to grow up. These wars naturally restricted the growth of trade and impoverished the whole country.

In 1573, however, one man, Oda Nobunaga, came to the fore in Japan. He became the *shōgun*, or military dictator, and within nine years had succeeded in gaining control of almost the whole of the country. When Nobunaga was assassinated in 1582, a commoner took over the government. Toyotomi Hideyoshi continued the work of unifying Japan, ruthlessly putting down any traces of insurrection. He revived the old gulf between the warriors of Japan — the *samurai* — and the commoners by introducing restrictions on the wearing of swords. 'Hideyoshi's sword-hunt', as it was known, meant that only samurai were allowed to wear two swords; the short one which everyone could wear and the long one which distinguished the samurai from the rest of the population.

Although Hideyoshi did much to settle Japan and increase trade with the outside world, by the time of his death in 1598 internal disturbances still had not been completely eliminated. The real isolation and unification of Japan began with the inauguration of the great Tokugawa rule. Tokugawa Ieyasu, a former associate of both Hideyoshi and Nobunaga, formally became the shōgun of Japan after defeating Hideyoshi's son Hideyori at the Battle of Sekigahara in 1600. Ieyasu established his government at Edo, present-day Tokyo, where he had a huge castle. His was a stable, peaceful government which began a period of Japanese history that lasted until the Imperial Restoration of 1868, for although Ieyasu died in 1616, members of his family succeeded one another and the title shōgun became virtually hereditary for the Tokugawas.

Ieyasu was determined to ensure his family's dictatorship. To this end, he paid lip service to the emperor in Kyoto, who remained the titular head of Japan, while curtailing his duties and involvement in the government. The real threat to Ieyasu's position could only come from the lords, and he effectively decreased their opportunities for revolt by devising schemes whereby all lords had to live in Edo for alternate years and by placing great restrictions on travelling. He allotted land in exchange for oaths of allegiance, and gave the provincial castles around Edo to members of his own family. He also employed a network of secret police and assassins.

A RIGID CLASS STRUCTURE

The Tokugawa period marks a great change in the social history of Japan. The bureaucracy of the Tokugawas was all-pervading. Not only were education, law, government and social class controlled, but even the costume and behaviour of each class. The traditional class consciousness of Japan hardened into a rigid class structure. There were basically four classes of person: samurai, farmers, artisans and merchants. The samurai were the highest — in esteem, if not in wealth — and included the lords, senior government officials, warriors, and minor officials and foot soldiers. Next in the hierarchy came the farmers, not because they were

well thought of, but because they provided the essential rice crops. Their lot was a rather unhappy one, as they were forced to give most of their crops to the lords and were not allowed to leave their farms. Then came the artisans and craftsmen, and last of all the merchants, who, though looked down upon, eventually rose to prominence because of the vast wealth they accumulated. Few people were outside this rigid hierarchy.

Musashi belonged to the samurai class. We find the origins of the samurai class in the *Kondei* ('stalwart youth') system established in AD 792, whereby the Japanese army – which had until then consisted mainly of spear-wielding foot soldiers – was revived by stiffening the ranks with permanent training officers recruited from among the young sons of the high families. These officers were mounted, wore armour, and used the bow and sword. In AD 782 the Emperor Kammu started to build Kyoto, where he constructed a training hall which exists to this day called the *Butokuden*, meaning 'Hall of the virtues of war'. Within a few years of this revival, the fierce Ainu, the aboriginal inhabitants of Japan who had until then confounded the army's attempt to move them from their ancestral lands, were driven far off to the northern island, Hokkaido.

THE RONIN

When the great provincial armies were gradually disbanded under Hideyoshi and Ieyasu, many out-of-work samurai roamed the country redundant in an era of peace. Musashi was one such samurai, a *rōnin* or 'wave man'. There were still samurai retainers to the Tokugawas and provincial lords, but their numbers were few. The hordes of redundant samurai found themselves living in a society which was completely based on the old chivalry, but at the same time they were apart from a society in which there was no place for men at arms. They became an inverted class, keeping the old chivalry alive by devotion to military arts with the fervour only Japanese possess. This was the time of the flowering of the sword arts, or Kendo.

Kendo – the Way of the sword – had long been synonymous with nobility in Japan. Since the founding of the samurai class in the eighth century, the military arts had become the highest form of study, inspired by the teachings of Zen and Shinto.

KENDO SCHOOLS

Schools of Kendo born in the early Muromachi period (approximately 1390 to 1600) were continued through the upheavals of the formation of the peaceful Tokugawa shōgunate, and survive to this day. The education of the sons of the Tokugawa shōguns was by means of schooling in the Chinese classics and fencing exercises. Where a Westerner might say, 'The pen is mightier than the sword', the Japanese would say, 'Bunbu ichi', or 'Pen and sword in accord'. Today, prominent businessmen and political figures in Japan still practise the old traditions of Kendo schools, preserving the forms of several hundred years ago.

To sum up, Musashi was a rōnin at a time when the samurai were formally considered to be the elite but actually had no means of livelihood unless they owned lands and castles. Many rōnin put up their swords and became artisans, but others, like Musashi, pursued the ideal of the warrior searching for enlightenment through the perilous paths of Kendo. Duels of revenge and tests of skill were commonplace and fencing schools multiplied. Two schools especially, the *Ittō* and the *Yagyū*, were sponsored by the Tokugawas. The Ittō school provided an unbroken line of Kendo teachers, and the Yagyū school eventually became the secret police of the Tokugawa bureaucracy.

DŌJŌ

Traditionally, the fencing halls of Japan, called *dōjō*, were associated with shrines and temples, but during Musashi's lifetime numerous schools sprang up in the new castle towns. Each daimyō, or lord, sponsored a Kendo school where his retainers could be trained and his sons educated. The hope of every rōnin was that he would defeat the students and master of a dōjō in combat, thus increasing his fame and bringing his name to the ears of one who might employ him.

The samurai wore two swords thrust through the belt with the cutting edge uppermost. The longer sword was carried out of doors only, while the shorter sword was worn at all times. For training, wooden or bamboo swords were often used. Duelling and other tests of arms were common, with both real and practice swords. These took place in fencing halls and before shrines, in the streets and within castle walls. Duels were fought to the death or until one of the contestants was disabled, but a few generations after Musashi's time the *shinai*, a pliable bamboo sword and, later, padded fencing armour came to be widely used, so the chances of injury were greatly reduced. The samurai studied with all kinds of weapons, including halberds, sticks, swords and chain-and-sickle. Many schools using such weapons survive in traditional form in Japan today.

To train in Kendo one must subjugate the self, bear the pain of gruelling practice, and cultivate a level mind in the face of peril. But the Way of the sword means not only fencing training but also living by the code of honour of the samurai elite. Warfare was the spirit of the samurai's everyday life, and he could face death as if it were a domestic routine. The meaning of life and death by the sword was mirrored in the everyday conduct of the feudal Japanese, and he who realized the resolute acceptance of death at any moment in his everyday life was a master of the sword. It is in order to attain such an understanding that later men have followed the ancient traditions of the sword-fencing styles, and even today give up their lives for Kendo practice.

MORAL TEACHING

The Way of the sword is the moral teaching of the samurai, fostered by the Confucianist philosophy which shaped the Tokugawa system, together with the native Shinto religion of Japan. From the Kamakura period to the Muromachi period, the warrior courts of Japan encouraged the austere Zen study among the samurai, and Zen went hand in hand with the arts of war. In Zen there are no elaborations; it aims directly at the true nature of things. There are no ceremonies, no teachings – the prize of Zen is essentially personal. Enlightenment in Zen does not mean a change in behaviour, but realization of the nature of ordinary life. The end point is the beginning, and the great virtue is simplicity. The secret teaching of the *Ittō-ryū* school of Kendo, *Kiri-otoshi*, is the first technique of some hundred or so. The teaching is *Ai Uchi*, meaning to cut the opponent just as he cuts you. This is the ultimate timing – it is lack of anger. It means to treat your enemy as an honoured guest. It also means to abandon your life or throw away fear.

The first technique is the last; the beginner and the master behave in the same way. Knowledge is a full circle. The first of Musashi's chapter headings

is 'Ground', for the basis of Kendo and Zen, and the last is 'Void', for that understanding which can only be expressed as nothingness. The teachings of Kendo are like the fierce verbal forays to which the Zen student is subjected. Assailed with doubts and misery, his mind and spirit in a whirl, the student is gradually guided to realization and understanding by his teacher. The Kendo student practises furiously, thousands of cuts morning and night, learning fierce techniques of horrible war, until eventually sword becomes 'no sword', intention becomes 'no intention', a spontaneous knowledge of every situation. The first elementary teaching becomes the highest knowledge, and the master still continues to practise this simple training, his every prayer.

Concerning the life of Miyamoto Musashi

Shinmen Musashi no Kami Fujiwara no Genshin, better known as Miyamoto Musashi, was born in a village called Miyamoto in the province Mimasaka in 1584. 'Musashi' is the name of an area southwest of Tokyo, and the appellation 'no Kami' means noble person of the area, while 'Fujiwara' is the name of the noble family foremost in Japan over a thousand years ago.

Musashi's ancestors were a branch of the powerful Harima clan in Kyushu, the southern island of Japan. Hirada Shokan, his grandfather, was a retainer of Shinmen Iga no Kami Sudeshige, the lord of Takeyama castle. His lord thought highly of Hirada Shokan, who eventually married his master's daughter.

When Musashi was seven, his father, Munisai, either died or abandoned the child. As his mother had also died, Musashi was left in the care of an uncle on his mother's side, a priest. So we find Musashi an orphan during Hideyoshi's campaigns of unification, the son of a samurai in a violent, unhappy land.

AN AGGRESSIVE NATURE
He was a boisterous youth, strong-willed and physically large for his age. Whether he was urged to pursue Kendo by his uncle, or whether his aggressive

nature led him to it, we do not know, but it is recorded that he slew a man in single combat when he was just thirteen years old. The opponent was Arima Kihei, a samurai of the *Shintō-ryū* school of military arts, skilled with sword and spear. The boy threw the man to the ground, and beat him about the head with a stick when he tried to rise. Kihei died vomiting blood.

Musashi's next contest was at the age of sixteen, when he defeated Tadashima Akiyama. About this time, he left home to embark on the 'Warrior Pilgrimage', which saw him victorious in scores of contests and took him to war six times, until he finally settled down at the age of fifty, having reached the end of his search for reason. There must have been many rōnin travelling the country on similar expeditions, some alone like Musashi and some enjoying sponsorship, though not on the scale of the pilgrimage of the famous swordsman Tsukahara Bokuden, who had travelled with a retinue of more than one hundred men in the previous century.

This part of Musashi's life was spent living apart from society while he devoted himself with a ferocious single-mindedness to the search for enlightenment by the Way of the sword. Concerned only with perfecting his skill, he lived as men need not live, wandering over Japan lashed by the cold winds of winter, not dressing his hair, not taking a wife, nor following any profession save his study. It is said he never entered a bathtub lest he was caught unawares without a weapon, and that his appearance was uncouth and wretched.

In the Battle of Sekigahara which resulted in Ieyasu succeeding Hideyoshi as shōgun of Japan, Musashi joined the ranks of the Ashikaga army to fight against Ieyasu. He endured the terrible three days during which seventy thousand people died, and he survived the hunting down and massacre of the vanquished army.

He went up to Kyoto, the capital, when he was twenty-one. This was the scene of his vendetta against the Yoshioka family. The Yoshiokas had been fencing instructors to the Ashikaga house for generations. Later forbidden to teach Kendo by Lord Tokugawa, the family became dyers, and are dyers today. Munisai, Musashi's father, had been invited to Kyoto some years before by the shōgun, Ashikaga Yoshiaka. Munisai was a competent swordsman, and an expert with the *jitte*, a kind of iron truncheon with a tongue for catching sword blades. The story has it that Munisai fought three of the Yoshiokas, winning two of the duels, and perhaps this has some bearing on Musashi's behaviour towards the family.

SWORDSMANSHIP

Yoshioka Seijiro, the head of the family, was the first to fight Musashi, on the moor outside the city. Seijiro was armed with a real sword and Musashi with a wooden sword. Musashi laid Seijiro out with a fierce attack and beat him savagely as he lay on the ground. The retainers carried their lord home on a rain-shutter, where for shame he cut off his samurai topknot.

Musashi lingered on in the capital, and his continued presence further irked the Yoshiokas. The second brother, Denshichiro, applied to Musashi for a duel. As a military ploy, Musashi arrived late on the appointed day and, seconds after the start of the fight, broke his opponent's skull with one blow of his wooden sword, killing Denshichiro outright.

The house issued yet another challenge with Hanshichiro, the young son of Seijiro, as champion. Hanshichiro was a mere boy, not yet in his teens. The contest was to be held near a pine tree adjacent to rice fields. Musashi arrived at the meeting place well before the appointed time and waited in hiding for his enemy to come. The child arrived dressed formally in war gear, with a party of well-armed retainers, determined to do away with Musashi. Musashi waited concealed in the shadows; just as they were thinking he had thought better of it and had decided to leave Kyoto, Musashi suddenly appeared in the midst of them and cut the boy down. Then, drawing both swords, he cut a path through the entourage and made his escape.

After that frightful episode, Musashi wandered over Japan becoming a legend in his own time. We find mention of his name and stories of his prowess in registers, diaries and on monuments, and in folk memory from Tokyo to Kyushu. He had more than sixty contests before he was twenty-nine, and won them all. The earliest account of his contests appears in *Niten Ki*, or 'Two Heavens Chronicle', a record compiled by his pupils a generation after his death.

In the year of the Yoshioka affair, 1605, he visited the temple *Ittō-ryū* Hōzōin in the south of the capital. Here he had a contest with Oku Hōzōin, the Nichiren sect pupil of the Zen priest Hoin Inei. The priest was a spearman, but no match for Musashi who defeated him twice with his short wooden sword. Musashi stayed at the temple for some time, studying fighting techniques and enjoying talks with the priests. There is still today a traditional spear-fighting form practised by the monks of Hōzōin. It is interesting that in ancient times the word *Osho*, which now means priest, used to mean 'spear teacher'. Hoin Inei was pupil to Izumi Musashi no Kami, a master of Shinto Kendo. The priest used spears with cross-shaped blades kept outside the temple under the eaves and used in fire-fighting.

When Musashi was in Iga province, he met a skilled chain-and-sickle fighter named Shishido Baikin. As Shishido twirled his chain, Musashi drew a dagger and pierced his breast, advancing to finish him off. The watching pupils attacked Musashi but he frightened them away in four directions.

In Edo, a fighter named Muso Gonosuke visited Musashi requesting a duel. At the time Musashi was cutting wood to make a bow and, granting Gonosuke's request, stood up, intending to use the slender wand he was cutting as a sword. Gonosuke made a fierce attack, but Musashi stepped straight in and banged him on the head. Gonosuke retreated.

Passing through Izumo province, Musashi visited Lord Matsudaira and asked permission to fight with his strongest expert. There were many good strategists in Izumo. Permission was granted against a man who used a 2.4m (8ft) long hexagonal wooden pole. The contest was held in the lord's library garden. Musashi used two wooden swords. He chased the samurai up the two wooden steps of the library veranda, thrust at his face on the second step, and hit him on both his arms as he flinched away. To the surprise of the assembled retainers, Lord Matsudaira asked Musashi to fight him. Musashi drove the lord up the library steps as before, and when the lord tried to make a resolute fencing attitude, Musashi hit his sword, with the words, 'fire and stones cut', breaking it in two. The lord bowed in defeat and Musashi stayed for some time as his teacher.

'SWALLOW COUNTER'

Musashi's most well-known duel was in the seventeenth year of Keicho, 1612, when he was in Ogura in Bunzen province. His opponent was Sasaki Kojiro, a young man who had developed a strong fencing technique known as *Tsubame-gaeshi* or 'swallow counter', inspired by the motion of a swallow's tail in flight. Kojiro was retained by the lord of the province, Hosokawa Tadaoki. Through the offices of Nagaoka Sato Okinaga, one of the Hosokawa retainers who had been a pupil of Musashi's father, Musashi applied to Tadaoki for permission to fight Kojiro. Permission was granted for the contest to be held at eight o'clock the next morning, and the place was to be an island some few miles from Ogura. That night, Musashi left his lodging and moved to the house of Kobayashi Tare Zaemon. This inspired a rumour that awe of Kojiro's subtle technique had made Musashi run away, afraid for his life.

The next day at eight o'clock Musashi could not be woken until a prompter came from the officials assembled on the island. He rose, drank the water they brought to him to wash with, and went straight down to the shore. As Sato rowed across to the island, Musashi fashioned a paper string to tie back the

sleeves of his kimono, and cut a wooden sword from the spare oar. When he had done this, he lay down to rest.

The boat neared the place of combat; Kojiro and the waiting officials were astounded to see the strange figure of Musashi, with his unkempt hair tied up in a towel, leap from the boat brandishing the long wooden oar and rush through the waves up the beach towards his enemy. Kojiro drew his long sword, a fine blade by Nagamitsu of Bizen, and threw away his scabbard. 'You have no more need of that,' said Musashi as he rushed forward with his sword held to one side. Kojiro was provoked into making the first cut and Musashi dashed upward at his blade, bringing the oar down on Kojiro's head. Musashi noted Kojiro's condition and bowed to the astounded officials before running back to his boat. Some sources have it that after he killed Kojiro, Musashi threw down the oar and, nimbly leaping back several paces, drew both his swords and flourished them with a shout at his fallen enemy.

In 1614, and again in 1615, he took the opportunity of once more experiencing warfare and siege. Ieyasu laid siege to Osaka castle, where the supporters of the Ashikaga family were gathered in insurrection. Musashi joined the Tokugawa forces in both winter and summer campaigns, now fighting against those he had fought for as a youth at Sekigahara.

According to his own writing, he came to understand strategy when he was fifty or fifty-one, in 1634. He and his adopted son Iori, a waif he had met in Dewa province on his travels, settled in Ogura in this year. Musashi was never again to leave Kyushu island. The Hosokawa house had been entrusted with the command of the hot seat of Higo province, Kumamoto castle, and the new lord of Bunzen was an Ogasawara.

Iori found employment under Ogasawara Tadazane, and as a captain in Tadazane's army fought against the Christians in the Shimabara uprising of 1638. The lords of the southern provinces had always been antagonistic to the Tokugawas and were the instigators of intrigue with foreign powers and the Japanese Christians. Musashi was a member of the field staff at Shimabara, where the Christians were massacred. After this, Ieyasu closed the ports of Japan to foreign intercourse, and they remained closed for more than two hundred years.

After six years in Ogura, Musashi was invited to stay with Churi, the Hosokawa lord of Kumamoto castle, as a guest. He stayed a few years with Lord Churi and spent his time teaching and painting. In 1643, he retired to a life of seclusion in a cave called Reigendo. Here he wrote *The Book of Five Rings*, addressed to his pupil Teruo Nobuyuki, a few weeks before his death on 19 May 1645.

Musashi is known to the Japanese as Kensei, that is, 'sword saint'. *The Book of Five Rings* is unique among books on martial art and heads every Kendo bibliography. It deals with the strategy of warfare and the methods of single combat in exactly the same way. It is, in Musashi's words, 'a guide for men who want to learn strategy', and is Musashi's last will, the key to the path he trod. When, at twenty-eight or twenty-nine, he had become such a strong fighter, he did not settle down and build a school, replete with success, but became doubly engrossed with his study. In his last days even, he scorned the life of comfort with Lord Hosokawa and lived two years alone in a mountain cave, deep in contemplation.

Musashi wrote, 'When you have attained the Way of strategy there will be not one thing that you cannot understand' and 'You will see the Way in everything.' He also produced masterpieces of ink painting, works in metal, and founded a school of sword-guard makers. His paintings are sometimes impressed with his seal, 'Musashi', or his *nom de plume* 'Niten'. Niten means 'Two Heavens', said by some to allude to his fighting attitude with a sword in each hand held above his head.

He wrote 'Study the Ways of all professions' and it is evident that he did just this. He sought out not only great swordsmen but also priests, strategists, artists and craftsmen, eager to broaden his knowledge.

Musashi writes about the various aspects of Kendo in such a way that it is possible for the beginner to study at beginner's level and for Kendo masters to study the same words on a higher level. This applies not just to military strategy, but to any situation where plans and tactics are used. Japanese businessmen have used *The Book of Five Rings* as a guide for business practice, turning sales campaigns into military operations by employing the same energetic methods.

Musashi's life study is thus as relevant in the twentieth century as it was on the medieval battleground and applies not just to the Japanese, but to all nations. I suppose you could sum up his inspiration as 'humility and hard work'.

Victor Harris

Preface

I have been many years training in the Way[1] of strategy, called *Niten Ichi Ryu*, and now I think I will explain it in writing for the first time.

It is now during the first ten days of the tenth month in the twentieth year of Kanei (1645). I have climbed mountain Iwato of Higo in Kyushu to pay homage to heaven[2], pray to Kwannon[3], and kneel before Buddha. I am a warrior of Harima province, Shinmen Musashi no Kami Fujiwara no Geshin, age sixty years.

From youth, my heart has been inclined toward the Way of strategy. My first duel was when I was thirteen; I struck down a strategist of the Shinto school, one Arima Kihei. When I was sixteen, I struck down an able strategist, Tadashima Akiyama. When I was twenty-one, I went up to the capital and met all manner of strategists, never once failing to win in many contests.

After that I went from province to province, duelling with strategists of various schools, and not once failed to win even though I had as many as sixty encounters. This was between the ages of thirteen and twenty-eight or twenty-nine. When I reached thirty, I looked back on my past. The previous victories were not due to my having mastered strategy. Perhaps it was natural ability, or the order of heaven, or that other schools' strategy was inferior.

After that, I studied morning and evening, searching for the principle, and came to realize the Way of strategy when I was fifty. Since then I have lived without following any particular Way. Thus, with the virtue of strategy, I practise many arts and abilities – all things with no teacher. To write this book I did not use the law of Buddha or the teachings of Confucius, neither old war chronicles nor books on martial tactics. I take up my brush to explain the true spirit of this Ichi school as it is mirrored in the Way of heaven and Kwannon. The time is the night of the tenth day of the tenth month, at the hour of the tiger (3–5 am).[4]

CHAPTER ONE

The Ground Book

Strategy is the craft of the warrior. Commanders must enact the craft, and troopers should know this Way. There is no warrior in the world today who really understands the Way of strategy.

There are various Ways. There is the Way of salvation by the law of Buddha, the Way of Confucius governing the Way of learning, the Way of healing as a doctor, as a poet teaching the Way of Waka,[5] tea, archery,[6] and many arts and skills. Each man practises as he feels inclined. It is said that the warrior's is the twofold Way of pen and sword,[7] and he should have a taste for both Ways.

Even if a man has no natural ability, he can be a warrior by sticking assiduously to both divisions of the Way. Generally speaking, the Way of the warrior is resolute acceptance of death.[8] Although not only warriors but priests, women, peasants and lowlier folk have been known to die readily in the cause of duty or out of shame, this is a different thing. The warrior is different in that studying the Way of strategy is based on overcoming men. Through victory gained in crossing swords with individuals, or enjoining battle with large numbers, we can attain power and fame for ourselves or for our lord. This is the virtue of strategy.

THE WAY OF STRATEGY

In China and Japan, practitioners of the Way have been known as 'masters of strategy'. Warriors must learn this Way.

Recently there have been people getting on in the world as strategists, but they are usually just sword-fencers. The attendants of the Kashima Kantori shrines[9] of the province Hitachi received instruction from the gods, and made schools based on this teaching, travelling from country to country instructing men. This is the recent meaning of strategy.

In olden times, strategy was listed among the Ten Abilities and Seven Arts as a beneficial practice. It was certainly an art, but as beneficial practice it was not limited to sword-fencing. The true value of sword-fencing cannot be seen within the confines of sword-fencing technique.

If we look at the world, we see arts for sale. Men use equipment to sell their own selves. As if with the nut and the flower, the nut has become less than the flower. In this kind of Way of strategy, both those teaching and those learning the way are concerned with colouring and showing off their technique, trying to hasten the bloom of the flower. They speak of 'This Dōjō' and 'That Dōjō'. They are looking for profit. Someone once said, 'Immature strategy is the cause of grief'. That was a true saying.

THE FOUR WAYS

There are four Ways in which men pass through life: as gentlemen, farmers, artisans and merchants.

The Way of the farmer: using agricultural instruments, he sees springs through to autumns with an eye on the changes of season.

Second is the Way of the merchant. The winemaker obtains his ingredients and puts them to use to make his living. The Way of the merchant is always to live by taking profit. This is the Way of the merchant.

Thirdly the gentleman warrior, carrying the weaponry of his Way. The Way of the warrior is to master the virtue of his weapons. If a gentleman dislikes strategy he will not appreciate the benefit of weaponry, so must he not have a little taste for this?

Fourthly the Way of the artisan. The Way of the carpenter[10] is to become proficient in the use of his tools, first to lay his plans with a true measure and then perform his work according to plan. Thus, he passes through life.

These are the Four Ways – of the gentleman, the farmer, the artisan and the merchant.

COMPARING THE WAY OF THE CARPENTER TO STRATEGY

The comparison with carpentry is through the connection with houses. Houses of the nobility, houses of warriors, the Four Houses,[11] ruin of houses, thriving of houses, the style of the house, the tradition of the house, and the name of the house. The carpenter uses a master plan of the building, and the Way of strategy is similar in that there is a plan of campaign. If you want to learn the craft of war, ponder over this book. The teacher is as a needle, the disciple is as thread. You must practise constantly.

Like the foreman carpenter, the commander must know natural rules, and the rules of the country, and the rules of houses. This is the Way of the foreman.

The foreman carpenter must know the architectural theory of towers and temples, and the plans of palaces, and must employ men to raise up houses. The Way of the foreman carpenter is the same as the Way of the commander of a warrior house.

In the construction of houses, choice of woods is made. Straight un-knotted timber of good appearance is used for the revealed pillars, straight timber with small defects is used for the inner pillars. Timber of the finest appearance, even if a little weak, is used for the thresholds, lintels, doors, and sliding doors,[12] and so on. Good, strong timber, though it be gnarled and knotted, can always be used discreetly in construction. Timber which is weak or knotted throughout should be used as scaffolding, and later for firewood.

The foreman carpenter allots his men work according to their ability. Floor layers, makers of sliding doors, thresholds and lintels, ceilings and so on. Those of lesser ability lay the floor joists, carve wedges and do such miscellaneous work. If the foreman knows and deploys his men well, the finished work will be good. The foreman should take into account the abilities and limitations of his men, circulating among them and asking nothing unreasonable. He should know their morale and spirit, and encourage them when necessary. This is the same as the principle of strategy.

THE WAY OF STRATEGY

Like a trooper, the carpenter sharpens his own tools. He carries his equipment in his tool box, and works under the direction of his foreman. He makes columns and girders with an axe, shapes floorboards and shelves with a plane, cuts fine openwork and carvings accurately, giving as excellent a finish as his skill will allow. This is the craft of the carpenters. When the carpenter grows to be skilled and understands measures, he can become a foreman.

The carpenter's attainment is, having tools which will cut well, to make small shrines,[13] writing shelves, tables, paper lanterns, chopping boards and pot-lids. These are the specialities of the carpenter. Things are similar for the trooper. You ought to think deeply about this.

The attainment of the carpenter is that his work is not warped, that the joints are not misaligned, and that the work is truly planed so that it meets well and is not merely finished in sections. This is essential. If you want to learn this Way, deeply consider the things written in this book one at a time. You must do sufficient research.

OUTLINE OF THE FIVE BOOKS OF THIS BOOK OF STRATEGY

The Way is shown in five books[14] concerning different aspects. These are Ground, Water, Fire, Tradition (Wind), and Void.[15]

The body of the Way of strategy from the viewpoint of my Ichi school is explained in the Ground Book. It is difficult to realize the true Way just through sword-fencing. Know the smallest things and the biggest things, the shallowest things and the deepest things. As if it were a straight road mapped out on the ground, the first book is called the Ground Book.

Second is the Water Book. With water as the basis, the spirit becomes like water. Water adopts the shape of its receptacle, it is sometimes a trickle and sometimes a wild sea. Water has a clear blue colour. By the clarity, things of Ichi school are shown in this book. If you master the principles of sword-fencing, when you freely beat one man, you beat any man in the world. The spirit of defeating a man is the same for ten million men. The strategist makes small things into big things, like building a great Buddha from a one-foot model. I

cannot write in detail how this is done. The principle of strategy is having one thing, to know ten thousand things. Things of the Ichi school are written in this, the Water Book.

Third is the Fire Book. This book is about fighting. The spirit of fire is fierce, whether the fire be small or big; and so it is with battles. The Way of battles is the same for man to man fights and for 10,000 a side battles. You must appreciate that spirit can become big or small. What is big is easy to perceive: what is small is difficult to perceive. In short, it is difficult for large numbers of men to change position, so their movements can be easily predicted. An individual can easily change his mind, so his movements are difficult to predict. You must appreciate this. The essence of this book is that you must train day and night in order to make quick decisions. In strategy, it is necessary to treat training as a part of normal life with your spirit unchanging. Thus, combat in battle is described in the Fire Book.

Fourthly the Wind Book. This book is not concerned with my Ichi school, but with other schools of strategy. By Wind, I mean old traditions, present-day traditions, and family traditions of strategy. Thus I clearly explain the strategies of the world. This is tradition. It is difficult to know yourself if you do not know others. To all Ways there are side tracks. If you study a Way daily, and your spirit diverges, you may think you are obeying a good way, but objectively it is not the true Way. If you are following the true Way and diverge a little, this will later become a large divergence. You must realize this. Other strategies have come to be thought of as mere sword-fencing, and it is not unreasonable that this should be so. The benefit of my strategy, although it includes sword-fencing, lies in a separate principle. I have explained what is commonly meant by strategy in other schools in the Tradition (Wind) Book (see page 77).

Fifthly, the Book of the Void. By Void, I mean that which has no beginning and no end. Attaining this principle means not attaining the principle. The Way of strategy is the Way of nature. When you appreciate the power of nature, knowing the rhythm of any situation, you will be able to hit the enemy naturally and strike naturally. All this is the Way of the Void. I intend to show how to follow the true Way according to nature in the Book of the Void.

NITEN ICHI RYU NI TO (ONE SCHOOL – TWO SWORDS)

Warriors, both commanders and troopers, carry two swords[16] at their belt. In olden times these were called the long sword and the sword; nowadays they are known as the sword and the companion sword. Let it suffice to say that in our land, whatever the reason, a warrior carries two swords at his belt. It is the Way of the warrior. Niten Ichi Ryu shows the advantage of using both swords.

The spear and halberd[17] are weapons which are carried out of doors. Students of the Ichi school Way of strategy should train from the start with the sword and long sword in either hand. This is the truth: when you sacrifice your life, you must make fullest use of your weaponry. It is false not to do so, and to die with a weapon yet undrawn.

If you hold a sword with both hands, it is difficult to wield it freely to left and right, so my method is to carry the sword in one hand. This does not apply to large weapons such as the spear or halberd, but swords and companion swords can be carried in one hand. It is encumbering to hold a sword in both hands when you are on horseback, when running on uneven roads, on swampy ground, muddy rice fields, stony ground, or in a crowd of people. To hold the long sword in both hands is not the true Way, for if you carry a bow or spear or other arms in your left hand you have only one hand free for the long sword. However, when it is difficult to cut an enemy down with one hand, you must use both hands. It is not difficult to wield a sword in one hand; the Way to learn this is to train with two long swords, one in each hand. It will seem difficult at first, but everything is difficult at first. Bows are difficult to draw, halberds are difficult to wield; as you become accustomed to the bow so your pull will become stronger. When you become used to wielding the long sword, you will gain the power of the Way and wield the sword well.

As I will explain in the second book, the Water Book, there is no fast way of wielding the long sword. The long sword should be wielded broadly, and the companion sword closely. This is the first thing to realize.

According to this Ichi school, you can win with a long weapon, and yet you can also win with a short weapon. In short, the Way of the Ichi school is the spirit of winning, whatever the weapon and whatever its size.

It is better to use two swords rather than one when you are fighting a crowd, and especially if you want to take a prisoner.

These things cannot be explained in detail. From one thing, know ten thousand things. When you attain the Way of strategy there will not be one thing you cannot see. You must study hard.

THE VIRTUE OF THE LONG SWORD

Masters of the long sword are called strategists. As for the other military arts, those who master the bow are called archers, those who master the spear are called spearmen, those who master the gun[18] are called marksmen, those who

master the halberd are called halberdiers. But we do not call masters of the Way of the long sword 'long-swordsmen', nor do we speak of 'companion-swordsmen'. Because bows, guns, spears and halberds are all warriors' equipment, they are certainly part of strategy. To master the virtue of the long sword is to govern the world and oneself, thus the long sword is the basis of strategy. The principle is 'strategy by means of the long sword'. If he attains the virtue of the long sword, one man can beat ten men. Just as one man can beat ten, so a hundred men can beat a thousand, and a thousand men can beat ten thousand. In my strategy, one man is the same as ten thousand, so this strategy is the complete warrior's craft.

The Way of the warrior does not include other Ways, such as Confucianism, Buddhism, certain traditions, artistic accomplishments and dancing.[19] But even though these are not part of the Way, if you know the Way broadly you will see it in everything. Men must polish their particular Way.

THE BENEFIT OF WEAPONS IN STRATEGY

There is a time and a place for use of weapons.

The best use of the companion sword is in a confined space, or when you are engaged closely with an opponent. The long sword can be used effectively in all situations.

The halberd is inferior to the spear on the battlefield. With the spear, you can take the initiative; the halberd is defensive. In the hands of one of two men of equal ability, the spear gives a little extra strength. Spear and halberd both have their uses, but neither is very beneficial in confined spaces. They cannot be used for taking a prisoner. They are essentially weapons for the field.

Anyway, if you learn 'indoor' techniques,[20] you will think narrowly and forget the true Way. Thus, you will have difficulty in actual encounters.

The bow is tactically strong at the commencement of battle, especially battles on a moor, as it is possible to shoot quickly from among the spearmen. However, it is unsatisfactory in sieges, or when the enemy is more than forty yards away. For this reason there are now few traditional schools of archery. There is little use today for this kind of skill.

From inside fortifications, the gun has no equal among weapons. It is the supreme weapon on the field before the ranks clash, but once swords are crossed

the gun becomes useless. One of the virtues of the bow is that you can see the arrows in flight and correct your aim accordingly, whereas gunshot cannot be seen. You must appreciate the importance of this.

Just as a horse must have endurance and no defects, so it is with weapons. Horses should walk strongly, and swords and companion swords should cut strongly. Spears and halberds must stand up to heavy use: bows and guns must be sturdy. Weapons should be hardy rather than decorative.

You should not have a favourite weapon. To become over-familiar with one weapon is as much a fault as not knowing it sufficiently well. You should not copy others, but use weapons which you can handle properly. It is bad for commanders and troopers to have likes and dislikes. These are things you must learn thoroughly.

TIMING IN STRATEGY

There is timing in everything. Timing in strategy cannot be mastered without a great deal of practice.

Timing is important in dancing and pipe or string music, for they are in rhythm only if timing is good. Timing and rhythm are also involved in the military arts, shooting bows and guns, and riding horses. In all skills and abilities there is timing. There is also timing in the Void.

There is timing in the whole life of the warrior, in his thriving and declining, in his harmony and discord. Similarly, there is timing in the Way of the merchant, in the rise and fall of capital. All things entail rising and falling timing. You must be able to discern this. In strategy, there are various timing considerations. From the outset, you must know the applicable timing and the inapplicable timing, and from among the large and small things and the fast and slow timings find the relevant timing, first seeing the distance timing and the background timing. This is the main thing in strategy. It is especially important to know the background timing, otherwise your strategy will become uncertain.

You win in battles with the timing in the Void born of the timing of cunning by knowing the enemies' timing, and thus using a timing which the enemy does not expect.

All the five books are chiefly concerned with timing. You must train sufficiently to appreciate all this.

If you practise day and night in the above Ichi school strategy, your spirit will naturally broaden. In this manner, large-scale strategy and the strategy of hand-to-hand combat is propagated in the world. This is recorded for the first time in the five books of Ground, Water, Fire, Tradition (Wind) and Void. This is the Way for men who want to learn my strategy:

1. Do not think dishonestly.
2. The Way is in training.
3. Become acquainted with every art.
4. Know the Ways of all professions.
5. Distinguish between gain and loss in worldly matters.
6. Develop intuitive judgement and understanding for everything.
7. Perceive those things which cannot be seen.
8. Pay attention even to trifles.
9. Do nothing which is of no use.

It is important to start by setting these broad principles in your heart, and train in the Way of strategy. If you do not look at things on a large scale it will be difficult for you to master strategy. If you learn and attain this strategy you will never lose even to twenty or thirty enemies. More than anything to start with you must set your heart on strategy and earnestly stick to the Way. You will come to be able actually to beat men in fights, and win with your eye. Also by training you will be able to control your own body freely, conquer men with your body, and with sufficient training you will be able to beat ten men with your spirit. When you have reached this point, will it not mean that you are invincible?

Moreover, in large-scale strategy the superior man will manage many subordinates dexterously, bear himself correctly, govern the country and foster the people, thus preserving the ruler's discipline. If there is a Way involving the spirit of not being defeated, to help oneself and gain honour, it is the Way of strategy.

CHAPTER TWO

The Water Book

The spirit of the Niten Ichi school of strategy is based on water, and this Water Book explains methods of victory as the long-sword form of the Ichi school. Language does not extend to explaining the Way in detail, but it can be grasped intuitively. Study this book; read a word then ponder on it. If you interpret the meaning loosely, you will mistake the Way.

The principles of strategy are written down here in terms of single combat, but you must think broadly so that you attain an understanding for ten-thousand-a-side battles.

Strategy is different from other things in that if you mistake the Way even a little you will become bewildered and fall into bad ways.

If you merely read this book you will not reach the Way of strategy. Absorb the things written in this book. Do not just read, memorize or imitate, but study hard so that you realize the principle from within your own heart and absorb these things into your body.

SPIRITUAL BEARING IN STRATEGY

In strategy, your spiritual bearing must not be any different from normal. Both in fighting and in everyday life you should be determined though calm. Meet the situation without tenseness yet not recklessly, your spirit settled yet unbiased. Even when your spirit is calm do not let your body relax, and when your body is relaxed do not let your spirit slacken. Do not let your spirit be influenced

by your body, or your body influenced by your spirit. Be neither insufficiently spirited nor over-spirited. An elevated spirit is weak and a low spirit is weak. Do not let the enemy see your spirit.

Small people must be completely familiar with the spirit of large people, and large people must be familiar with the spirit of small people. Whatever your size, do not be misled by the reactions of your own body. With your spirit open and unconstricted, look at things from a high point of view. You must cultivate your wisdom and spirit. Polish your wisdom: learn public justice, distinguish between good and evil, study the Ways of different arts one by one. When you cannot be deceived by men you will have realized the wisdom of strategy.

The wisdom of strategy is different from other things. On the battlefield, even when you are hard-pressed, you should ceaselessly research the principles of strategy so that you can develop a steady spirit.

STANCE IN STRATEGY

Adopt a stance with the head erect, neither hanging down, nor looking up, nor twisted. Your forehead and the space between your eyes should not be wrinkled. Do not roll your eyes nor allow them to blink, but slightly narrow them. With your features composed, keep the line of your nose straight with a feeling of slightly flaring your nostrils. Hold the line of the rear of the neck straight: instil vigour into your hairline, and in the same way from the shoulders down through your entire body. Lower both shoulders and, without the buttocks jutting out, put strength into your legs from the knees to the tops of your toes. Brace your abdomen so that you do not bend at the hips. Wedge your companion sword in your belt against your abdomen, so that your belt is not slack – this is called 'wedging in'.

In all forms of strategy, it is necessary to maintain the combat stance in everyday life and to make your everyday stance your combat stance. You must research this well.

THE GAZE IN STRATEGY

The gaze should be large and broad. This is the twofold gaze, 'perception and sight'. Perception is strong and sight is weak.

In strategy, it is important to see distant things as if they were close and to take a distanced view of close things. It is important in strategy to know the enemy's sword and not to be distracted by insignificant movements of his sword. You must study this. The gaze is the same for single combat and for large–scale combat.

It is necessary in strategy to be able to look to both sides without moving the eyeballs. You cannot master this ability quickly. Learn what is written here; use this gaze in everyday life and do not vary it whatever happens.

HOLDING THE LONG SWORD

Grip the long sword with a rather floating feeling in your thumb and forefinger, with the middle finger neither tight nor slack, and with the last two fingers tight. It is bad to have play in your hands.

When you take up a sword, you must feel intent on cutting the enemy. As you cut an enemy you must not change your grip, and your hands must not 'cower'. When you dash the enemy's sword aside, or ward it off, or force it down, you must slightly change the feeling in your thumb and forefinger. Above all, you must be intent on cutting the enemy in the way you grip the sword.

The grip for combat and for sword-testing[21] is the same. There is no such thing as a 'man–cutting grip'.

Generally, I dislike fixedness in both long swords and hands. Fixedness means a dead hand. Pliability is a living hand. You must bear this in mind.

FOOTWORK[22]

With the tips of your toes somewhat floating, tread firmly with your heels. Whether you move fast or slow, with large or small steps, your feet must always move as in normal walking. I dislike the three walking methods known as 'jumping-foot', 'floating-foot' and 'fixed-steps'.

So-called 'Yin-Yang foot' is important to the Way. Yin-Yang foot means not moving on only one foot. It means moving your feet left-right and right-left when cutting, withdrawing, or warding off a cut. You should not move on one foot preferentially.

THE FIVE ATTITUDES

The Five Attitudes are: Upper, Middle, Lower, Right Side and Left Side. These are the five. Although attitude has these five dimensions, the one purpose of all of them is to cut the enemy. There are none but these five attitudes.

Whatever attitude you are in, do not be conscious of making the attitude; think only of cutting. Your attitude should be large or small according to the situation. Upper, Lower and Middle attitudes are decisive. Left Side and Right Side attitudes are fluid. Left and Right attitudes should be used if there is an obstruction overhead or to one side. The decision to use Left or Right depends on the place.

The essence of the Way is this. To understand attitude, you must thoroughly understand the Middle attitude. The Middle attitude is the heart of the attitudes. If we look at strategy on a broad scale, the Middle attitude is the seat of the commander, with the other four attitudes following the commander. You must appreciate this.

THE WAY OF THE LONG SWORD

Knowing the Way of the long sword[23] means we can wield with two fingers the sword we usually carry. If we know the path of the sword well, we can wield it easily. If you try to wield the long sword quickly, you will mistake the Way. To wield the long sword well you must wield it calmly. If you try to wield it quickly, like a folding fan[24] or a short sword, you will err by using 'short sword chopping'. You cannot cut a man with a long sword using this method.

When you have cut downwards with the long sword, lift it straight upwards; when you cut sideways, return the sword along a sideways path. Return the sword in a reasonable way, always stretching the elbows broadly. Wield the sword strongly.

This is the Way of the long sword.

If you learn to use the five approaches of my strategy, you will be able to wield a sword well. You must train constantly.

THE FIVE APPROACHES

1. The first approach is the Middle attitude. Confront the enemy with the point of your sword against his face. When he attacks, dash his sword to the right and 'ride' it. Or, when the enemy attacks, deflect the point of his sword by hitting downwards, keeping your long sword where it is, and as the enemy renews the attack cut his arms from below. This is the first method.

    The five approaches are this kind of thing. You must train repeatedly using a long sword in order to learn them. When you master my Way of the long sword, you will be able to control any attack the enemy makes. I assure you, there are no attitudes other than the five attitudes of the long sword of Ni To.

2. In the second approach with the long sword, from the Upper attitude cut the enemy just as he attacks. If the enemy evades the cut, keep your sword where it is and, scooping from below, cut him as he renews the attack. It is possible to repeat the cut from here.

    In this method, there are various changes in timing and spirit. You will be able to understand this by training in the Ichi school. You will always win with the five long sword methods. You must train repeatedly.

3. In the third approach, adopt the Lower attitude, anticipating scooping up. When the enemy attacks, hit his hands from below. As you do so, he may try to hit your sword down. If this is the case, cut his upper arm(s) horizontally with a feeling of 'crossing'. This means that from the Lower attitudes you hit the enemy at the instant that he attacks.

    You will encounter this method often, both as a beginner and in later strategy. You must train holding a long sword.

4. In this fourth approach, adopt the Left Side attitude. As the enemy attacks, hit his hands from below. If, as you hit his hands, he attempts to dash down your sword, with the feeling of hitting his hands, parry the path of his long sword and cut across from above your shoulder. This is the Way of the Long

Sword, Through this Method, you win by parrying the line of the enemy's attack. You must study this.

5. In the fifth approach, the sword is in the Right Side attitude. In accordance with the enemy's attack, cross your sword from below at the side to the Upper attitude. Then cut straight from above. This method is essential for knowing the Way of the long sword well. If you can use this method, you can freely wield a heavy long sword.

    I cannot describe in detail how to use these five approaches. You must become well acquainted with my 'in harmony with the long sword' Way, learn large-scale timing, understand the enemy's long sword, and become used to the five approaches from the outset. You will always win by using these five methods, with various timing considerations discerning the enemy's spirit. You must consider all this carefully.

THE ATTITUDE–NO-ATTITUDE TEACHING

Attitude-No-Attitude means that there is no need for what are known as long sword attitudes.

Even so, attitudes exist as the five ways of holding the long sword. However you hold the sword, it must be in such a way that it is easy to cut the enemy well, in accordance with the situation, the place, and your relation to the enemy. From the Upper attitude, as your spirit lessens you can adopt the Middle attitude, and from the Middle attitude you can raise the sword a little in your technique and adopt the Upper attitude. From the Lower attitude, you can raise the sword a little and adopt the Middle attitudes as the occasion demands. According to the situation, if you turn your sword from either the Left Side or Right Side attitude towards the centre, the Middle or the Lower attitude results.

The principle of this is called 'Existing Attitude – Non-existing Attitude'.

The primary thing when you take a sword in your hands is your intention to cut the enemy, whatever the means. Whenever you parry, hit, spring, strike or touch the enemy's cutting sword, you must cut the enemy in the same movement. It is essential to attain this. If you think only of hitting, springing, striking or touching the enemy, you will not be able actually to cut him. More

than anything, you must be thinking of carrying your movement through to cutting him. You must thoroughly research this.

Attitude in strategy on a larger scale is called 'battle array'. Such attitudes are all for winning battles. Fixed formation is bad. Study this well.

TO HIT THE ENEMY 'IN ONE TIMING'

'In one timing' means, when you have closed with the enemy, to hit him as quickly and directly as possible, without moving your body or settling your spirit, while you see that he is still undecided. The timing of hitting before the enemy decides to withdraw, break or hit, is this 'in one timing'.

You must train to achieve this timing, to be able to hit in the timing of an instant.

THE 'ABDOMEN TIMING OF TWO'

When you attack and the enemy quickly retreats, as you see him tense you must feint a cut. Then, as he relaxes, follow up and hit him. This is the 'abdomen timing of two'.

It is very difficult to attain this merely by reading this book, but you will soon understand with a little instruction.

'NO DESIGN, NO CONCEPTION'[25]

In this method, when the enemy attacks and you also decide to attack, hit with your body, and hit with your spirit, and hit from the Void with your hands, accelerating strongly. This is the 'no design, no conception' cut.

This is the most important method of hitting. It is often used. You must train hard to understand it.

THE 'FLOWING WATER' CUT

The 'flowing water' cut is used when you are struggling blade to blade with the enemy. When he breaks and quickly withdraws, trying to spring with his long sword, expand your body and spirit and cut him as slowly as possible with your long sword, following your body like stagnant water. You can cut with certainty if you learn this. You must discern the enemy's grade.

THE 'CONTINUOUS' CUT

When you attack and the enemy also attacks and your swords spring together, in one action cut his head, hands and legs. When you cut several places with one sweep of the long sword, it is the 'continuous' cut. You must practise this cut; it is often used. With detailed practice you should be able to understand it.

THE 'FIRE AND STONES' CUT

The 'fire and stones' cut means that when the enemy's long sword and your long sword clash together, you cut as strongly as possible without raising the sword even a little. This means cutting quickly with the hands, body and legs – all three cutting strongly. If you train well enough you will be able to strike strongly.

THE 'RED LEAVES' CUT

The 'red leaves' cut (alluding to falling, dying leaves) means knocking down the enemy's long sword. The spirit should be getting control of his sword. When the enemy is in a long-sword attitude in front of you and intent on cutting, hitting and parrying, you strongly hit the enemy's sword with the 'fire and stones' cut, perhaps in the design of the 'no design, no conception' cut. If you then beat down the point of his sword with a sticky feeling, he will necessarily drop the sword. If you practise this cut, it becomes easy to make the enemy drop his sword. You must train repetitively.

THE 'BODY IN PLACE OF THE LONG SWORD'

Also the 'long sword in place of the body'. Usually we move the body and the sword at the same time to cut the enemy. However, according to the enemy's cutting method, you can dash against him with your body first, and afterwards cut with the sword. If his body is immovable, you can cut first with the long sword, but generally you hit first with the body and then cut with the long sword. You must research this well and practise hitting.

'CUT AND SLASH'

To 'cut and slash' are two different things. Cutting, whatever form of cutting it is, is decisive, with a resolute spirit. Slashing is nothing more than touching the enemy. Even if you slash strongly, and even if the enemy dies instantly, it is slashing. When you cut, your spirit is resolved. You must appreciate this. If you first slash the enemy's hands or legs, you must then cut strongly. Slashing is in spirit the same as touching. When you realize this, they become indistinguishable. Learn this well.

'CHINESE MONKEY'S BODY'

The 'Chinese monkey's body' is the spirit of not stretching out your arms. The spirit is to get in quickly, without in the least extending your arms, before the enemy cuts. If you are intent upon not stretching out your arms, you are effectively far away; the spirit is to go in with your whole body. When you come to within arm's reach it becomes easy to move your body in. You must research this well.

'GLUE AND LACQUER EMULSION BODY'[26]

The spirit of 'glue and lacquer emulsion body' is to stick to the enemy and not separate from him. When you approach the enemy, stick firmly with your head, body and legs. People tend to advance their head and legs quickly, but their body lags behind. You should stick firmly so that there is not the slightest gap between the enemy's body and your body. You must consider this carefully.

'TO STRIVE FOR HEIGHT'

By 'to strive for height' is meant, when you close with the enemy, to strive with him for superior height without cringing. Stretch your legs, stretch your hips, and stretch your neck face to face with him. When you think you have won, and you are the higher, thrust in strongly. You must learn this.

'TO APPLY STICKINESS'

When the enemy attacks and you also attack with the long sword, you should go in with a sticky feeling and fix your long sword against the enemy's as you receive his cut. The spirit of stickiness is not hitting very strongly, but hitting so that the long swords do not separate easily. It is best to approach as calmly as possible when hitting the enemy's long sword with stickiness. The difference

between 'stickiness' and 'entanglement' is that stickiness is firm and entanglement is weak. You must appreciate this.

THE 'BODY STRIKE'

The 'body strike' means to approach the enemy through a gap in his guard. The spirit is to strike him with your body. Turn your face a little aside and strike the enemy's breast with your left shoulder thrust out. Approach with a spirit of bouncing the enemy away, striking as strongly as possible in time with your breathing. If you achieve this method of closing with the enemy, you will be able to knock him ten or twenty feet away. It is possible to strike the enemy until he is dead. Train well.

THREE WAYS TO PARRY HIS ATTACK

There are three methods to parry a cut:

First, by dashing the enemy's long sword to your right, as if thrusting at his eyes, when he makes an attack;

Or to parry by thrusting the enemy's long sword towards his right eye with the feeling of snipping his neck;

Or, when you have a short 'long sword', without worrying about parrying the enemy's long sword, to close with him quickly, thrusting at his face with your left hand.

These are the three ways of parrying. You must bear in mind that you can always clench your left hand and thrust at the enemy's face with your fist. It is necessary to train well.

'TO STAB AT THE FACE'

'To stab at the face' means, when you are in confrontation with the enemy, that your spirit is intent on stabbing at his face, following the line of the blades with the point of your long sword. If you are intent on stabbing at his face, his face and body will become rideable. When the enemy becomes rideable, there are various opportunities for winning. You must concentrate on this. When fighting and the enemy's body becomes as if rideable, you can win quickly, so you ought

not to forget to stab at the face. You must pursue the value of this technique through training.

'TO STAB AT THE HEART'

'To stab at the heart' means, when fighting and there are obstructions above or to the sides, and whenever it is difficult to cut, to thrust at the enemy. You must stab the enemy's breast without letting the point of your long sword waver, showing the enemy the ridge of the blade square-on, and with the spirit of deflecting his long sword. The spirit of this principle is often useful when we become tired or for some reason our long sword will not cut. You must understand the application of this method.

'TO SCOLD "TUT-TUT!"'

'Scold' means that, when the enemy tries to counter-cut as you attack, you counter-cut again from below as if thrusting at him, trying to hold him down. With very quick timing you cut, scolding the enemy. Thrust up, 'Tut!', and cut 'TUT!' This timing is encountered time and time again in exchanges of blows. The way to scold Tut-TUT is to time the cut simultaneously with raising your long sword as if to thrust the enemy. You must learn this through repetitive practice.

THE 'SMACKING PARRY'

By 'smacking parry' is meant that when you clash swords with the enemy, you meet his attacking cut on your long sword with a tee-dum, tee-dum rhythm, smacking his sword and cutting him. The spirit of the smacking parry is not parrying, or smacking strongly, but smacking the enemy's long sword in accordance with his attacking cut, primarily intent on quickly cutting him. If you understand the timing of smacking, however hard your long swords clash together, your sword point will not be knocked back even a little. You must research sufficiently to realize this.

'THERE ARE MANY ENEMIES'

'There are many enemies'[27] applies when you are fighting one against many. Draw both sword and companion sword and assume a wide-stretched left and right attitude. The spirit is to chase the enemies around from side to side, even though they come from all four directions. Observe their attacking order, and go to meet first those who attack first. Sweep your eyes around broadly, carefully examining the attacking order, and cut left and right alternately with your swords. Waiting is bad. Always quickly reassume your attitudes to both sides, cut the enemies down as they advance, crushing them in the direction from which they attack. Whatever you do, you must drive the enemy together, as if tying a line of fishes, and when they are seen to be piled up, cut them down strongly without giving them room to move.

THE ADVANTAGE WHEN COMING TO BLOWS

You can know how to win through strategy with the long sword, but it cannot be clearly explained in writing. You must practise diligently in order to understand how to win.

Oral tradition[28]: 'The true Way of strategy is revealed in the long sword.'

'ONE CUT'

You can win with certainty with the spirit of 'one cut'. It is difficult to attain this if you do not learn strategy well. If you train well in this Way, strategy will come from your heart and you will be able to win at will. You must train diligently.

'DIRECT COMMUNICATION'

The spirit of 'direct communication' is how the true Way of the Nito Ichi school is received and handed down.

Oral tradition: 'Teach your body strategy.'

To learn how to win with the long sword in strategy, first learn the five approaches and the five attitudes, and absorb the Way of the long sword naturally in your body. You must understand spirit and timing, handle the long sword naturally, and move body and legs in harmony with your spirit. Whether beating one man or two, you will then know values in strategy.

Study the contents of this book, taking one item at a time, and through fighting with enemies you will gradually come to know the principle of the Way.

Deliberately, with a patient spirit, absorb the virtue of all this, from time to time raising your hand in combat. Maintain this spirit whenever you cross swords with an enemy.

Step by step walk the thousand-mile road.

Study strategy over the years and achieve the spirit of the warrior. Today is victory over yourself of yesterday; tomorrow is your victory over lesser men. Next, in order to beat more skilful men, train according to this book, not allowing your heart to be swayed along a side track. Even if you kill an enemy, if it is not based on what you have learned it is not the true Way.

If you attain this Way of victory, then you will be able to beat several tens of men. What remains is sword-fighting ability, which you can attain in battles and duels.

CHAPTER THREE

The Fire Book

*In this, the Fire Book of the
Nito Ichi school of strategy,
I describe fighting as fire.*

In the first place, people think narrowly about the benefit of strategy. By using only their fingertips, they only know the benefit of three of the five inches of the wrist. They let a contest be decided, as with the folding fan, merely by the span of their forearms. They specialize in the small matter of dexterity, learning such trifles as hand and leg movements with the bamboo practice sword.[29]

In my strategy, the training for killing enemies is by way of many contests, fighting for survival, discovering the meaning of life and death, learning the Way of the sword, judging the strength of attacks and understanding the Way of the 'edge and ridge' of the sword.

You cannot profit from small techniques, particularly when full armour[30] is worn. My Way of strategy is the sure method to win when fighting for your life one man against five or ten. There is nothing wrong with the principle 'one man can beat ten, so a thousand men can beat ten thousand'. You must research this. Of course, you cannot assemble a thousand or ten thousand men for everyday training. But you can become a master of strategy by training alone with a sword, so that you can understand the enemy's strategies, his strength and resources, and come to appreciate how to apply strategy to beat ten thousand enemies.

Any man who wants to master the essence of my strategy must research diligently, training morning and evening. Thus can he polish his skill, become free from self, and realize extraordinary ability. He will come to possess miraculous power.

This is the practical result of strategy.

DEPENDING ON THE PLACE

Examine your environment.

Stand in the sun; that is, take up an attitude with the sun behind you. If the situation does not allow this, you must try to keep the sun on your right side. In buildings, you must stand with the entrance behind you or to your right. Make sure that your rear is unobstructed, and that there is free space on your left, your right side being occupied with your sword attitude. At night, if the enemy can be seen, keep the fire behind you and the entrance to your right, and otherwise take up your attitude as above. You must look down on the enemy, and take up your attitude on slightly higher places. For example, the Kamiza[31] in a house is thought of as a high place.

When the fight comes, always endeavour to chase the enemy around to your left side. Chase him towards awkward places, and try to keep him with his back to awkward places. When the enemy gets into an inconvenient position, do not let him look around, but conscientiously chase him around and pin him down. In houses, chase the enemy into the thresholds, lintels, doors, verandas, pillars, and so on, again not letting him see his situation.

Always chase the enemy into bad footholds, obstacles at the side, and so on, using the virtues of the place to establish predominant positions from which to fight. You must research and train diligently in this.

THE THREE METHODS TO FORESTALL THE ENEMY[32]

The first is to forestall him by attacking. This is called *Ken No Sen* (to set him up).

Another method is to forestall him as he attacks. This is called *Tai No Sen* (to wait for the initiative).

The other method is when you and the enemy attack together. This is called *Tai Tai No Sen* (to accompany him and forestall him).

There are no methods of taking the lead other than these three. Because you can win quickly by taking the lead, it is one of the most important things in strategy. There are several things involved in taking the lead. You must make the best of the situation, see through the enemy's spirit so that you grasp his strategy and defeat him. It is impossible to write about this in detail.

THE FIRST – KEN NO SEN

When you decide to attack, keep calm and dash in quickly, forestalling the enemy. Or you can advance seemingly strongly but with a reserved spirit, forestalling him with the reserve.

Alternatively, advance with as strong a spirit as possible, and when you reach the enemy move with your feet a little quicker than normal, unsettling him and overwhelming him sharply.

Or, with your spirit calm, attack with a feeling of constantly crushing the enemy, from first to last. The spirit is to win in the depths of the enemy.

These are all Ken No Sen.

THE SECOND – TAI NO SEN

When the enemy attacks, remain undisturbed but feign weakness. As the enemy reaches you, suddenly move away indicating that you intend to jump aside, then dash in attacking strongly as soon as you see the enemy relax. This is one way.

Or, as the enemy attacks, attack more strongly, taking advantage of the resulting disorder in his timing to win.

This is the Tai No Sen principle.

THE THIRD – TAI TAI NO SEN

When the enemy makes a quick attack, you must attack strongly and calmly, aim for his weak point as he draws near, and strongly defeat him.

Or, if the enemy attacks calmly, you must observe his movement and, with your body rather floating, join in with his movements as he draws near. Move quickly and cut him strongly.

This is Tai Tai No Sen.

These things cannot be clearly explained in words. You must research what is written here. In these three ways of forestalling, you must judge the situation. This does not mean that you always attack first; but if the enemy attacks first you can lead him around. In strategy, you have effectively won when you forestall the enemy, so you must train well to attain this.

'TO HOLD DOWN A PILLOW'

'To hold down a pillow' means not allowing the enemy's head to rise.

In contests of strategy, it is bad to be led about by the enemy. You must always be able to lead the enemy about. Obviously, the enemy will also be thinking of doing this, but he cannot forestall you if you do not allow him to come out. In strategy, you must stop the enemy as he attempts to cut; you must push down his thrust, and throw off his hold when he tries to grapple. This is the meaning of 'to hold down a pillow'. When you have grasped this principle, whatever the enemy tries to bring about in the fight you will see in advance and suppress it. The spirit is to check his attack at the syllable 'at . . .'; when he jumps, check his advance at the syllable 'ju . . .'; and check his cut at 'cu . . .'.

The important thing in strategy is to suppress the enemy's useful actions but allow his useless actions. However, doing this alone is defensive. First, you must act according to the Way, suppress the enemy's techniques, foil his plans, and thence command him directly. When you can do this, you will be a master of strategy. You must train well and research 'holding down a pillow'.

'CROSSING AT A FORD'

'Crossing at a ford' means, for example, crossing the sea at a strait, or crossing over a hundred miles of broad sea at a crossing place. I believe this 'crossing at a ford' occurs often in a man's lifetime. It means setting sail even though your friends stay in harbour, knowing the route, knowing the soundness of your ship and the favour of the day. When all the conditions are met, and there is perhaps a favourable wind, or a tailwind, then set sail. If the wind changes within a few miles of your destination, you must row across the remaining distance without sail.

If you attain this spirit, it applies to everyday life. You must always think of crossing at a ford.

In strategy, also, it is important to 'cross at a ford'. Discern the enemy's capability and, knowing your own strong points, 'cross the ford' at the advantageous place, as a good captain crosses a sea route. If you succeed in crossing at the best place, you may take your ease. To cross at a ford means to attack the enemy's weak point, and to put yourself in an advantageous position. This is how to win in large-scale strategy. The spirit of crossing at a ford is necessary in both large- and small-scale strategy.

You must research this well.

'TO KNOW THE TIMES'

'To know the times' means to know the enemy's disposition in battle. Is it flourishing or waning? By observing the spirit of the enemy's men and getting the best position, you can work out the enemy's disposition and move your men accordingly. You can win through this principle of strategy, fighting from a position of advantage.

When in a duel, you must forestall the enemy and attack when you have first recognized his school of strategy, perceived his quality and his strong and weak

points. Attack in an unsuspected manner, knowing his metre and modulation and the appropriate timing.

Knowing the times means, if your ability is high, seeing right into things. If you are thoroughly conversant with strategy, you will recognize the enemy's intentions and thus have many opportunities to win. You must sufficiently study this.

'TO TREAD DOWN THE SWORD'

'To tread down the sword' is a principle often used in strategy. First, in large-scale strategy, when the enemy first discharges bows and guns and then attacks, it is difficult for us to attack if we are busy loading powder into our guns or notching our arrows. The spirit is to attack quickly while the enemy is still shooting with bows or guns. The spirit is to win by 'treading down' as we receive the enemy's attack.

In single combat, we cannot get a decisive victory by cutting, with a 'tee-dum, tee-dum' feeling, in the wake of the enemy's attacking long sword. We must defeat him at the start of his attack, in the spirit of treading him down with the feet, so that he cannot rise again to the attack.

'Treading' does not simply mean treading with the feet. Tread with the body, tread with the spirit, and, of course, tread and cut with the long sword. You must achieve the spirit of not allowing the enemy to attack a second time. This is the spirit of forestalling in every sense. Once at the enemy, you should not aspire just to strike him, but to cling after the attack. You must study this deeply.

TO KNOW 'COLLAPSE'

Everything can collapse. Houses, bodies, and enemies collapse when their rhythm becomes deranged.

In large-scale strategy, when the enemy starts to collapse, you must pursue him without letting the chance go. If you fail to take advantage of your enemies' collapse, they may recover.

In single combat, the enemy sometimes loses timing and collapses. If you let this opportunity pass, he may recover and not be so negligent thereafter. Fix your eye on the enemy's collapse, and chase him, attacking so that you do not let him recover. You must do this. The chasing attack is with a strong spirit. You must utterly cut the enemy down so that he does not recover his position. You must understand utterly how to cut down the enemy.

'TO BECOME THE ENEMY'

'To become the enemy' means to think yourself into the enemy's position. In the world, people tend to think of a robber trapped in a house as a fortified enemy. However, if we think of 'becoming the enemy', we feel that the whole world is against us and that there is no escape. He who is shut inside is a pheasant. He who enters to arrest is a hawk. You must appreciate this.

In large-scale strategy, people are always under the impression that the enemy is strong, and so tend to become cautious. But if you have good soldiers, and if you understand the principles of strategy, and if you know how to beat the enemy, there is nothing to worry about.

In single combat, also, you must put yourself in the enemy's position. If you think, 'Here is a master of the Way, who knows the principles of strategy', then you will surely lose. You must consider this deeply.

'TO RELEASE FOUR HANDS'

'To release four hands'[33] is used when you and the enemy are contending with the same spirit, and the issue cannot be decided. Abandon this spirit and win through an alternative resource.

In large-scale strategy, when there is a 'four hands' spirit, do not give up – it is man's existence. Immediately throw away this spirit and win with a technique the enemy does not expect.

In single combat also, when we think we have fallen into the 'four hands' situation, we must defeat the enemy by changing our mind and applying a suitable technique according to his condition. You must be able to judge this.

'TO MOVE THE SHADOW'

'To move the shadow' is used when you cannot see the enemy's spirit.

In large-scale strategy, when you cannot see the enemy's position, indicate that you are about to attack strongly, to discover his resources. It is easy then to defeat him with a different method once you see his resources.

In single combat, if the enemy takes up a rear or side attitude of the long sword so that you cannot see his intention, make a feint attack, and the enemy will show his long sword, thinking he sees your spirit. Benefitting from what you are shown, you can win with certainty. If you are negligent, you will miss the timing. Research this well.

'TO HOLD DOWN A SHADOW'

'Holding down a shadow' is used when you can see the enemy's attacking spirit.

In large-scale strategy, when the enemy embarks on an attack, if you make a show of strongly suppressing his technique, he will change his mind. Then, altering your spirit, defeat him by forestalling him with a Void spirit.

Or, in single combat, hold down the enemy's strong intention with a suitable timing, and defeat him by forestalling him with this timing. You must study this well.

TO PASS ON

Many things are said to be passed on. Sleepiness can be passed on, and yawning can be passed on. Time can be passed on also.

In large-scale strategy, when the enemy is agitated and shows an inclination to rush, do not mind in the least. Make a show of complete calmness, and the enemy will be taken by this and will become relaxed. When you see that this spirit has been passed on, you can bring about the enemy's defeat by attacking strongly with a Void spirit.

In single combat, you can win by relaxing your body and spirit and then, catching on the moment the enemy relaxes, attack strongly and quickly, forestalling him.

What is known as 'getting someone drunk' is similar to this. You can also infect the enemy with a bored, careless, or weak spirit. You must study this well.

TO CAUSE LOSS OF BALANCE

Many things can cause a loss of balance. One cause is danger, another is hardship, and another is surprise. You must research this.

In large-scale strategy, it is important to cause loss of balance. Attack without warning where the enemy is not expecting it, and while his spirit is undecided follow up your advantage and, having the lead, defeat him.

Or, in single combat, start by making a show of being slow, then suddenly attack strongly. Without allowing him space for breath to recover from the fluctuation of spirit, you must grasp the opportunity to win. Get the feel of this.

TO FRIGHTEN

Fright often occurs, caused by the unexpected.

In large-scale strategy, you can frighten the enemy not by what you present to their eyes, but by shouting, making a small force seem large, or by threatening

them from the flank without warning. These things all frighten. You can win by making best use of the enemy's frightened rhythm.

In single combat, also, you must use the advantage of taking the enemy unawares by frightening him with your body, long sword, or voice, to defeat him. You should research this well.

'TO SOAK IN'

When you have come to grips, and are striving together with the enemy, and you realize that you cannot advance, you 'soak in' and become one with the enemy. You can win by applying a suitable technique while you are mutually entangled.

In battles involving large numbers as well as in fights with small numbers, you can often win decisively with the advantage of knowing how to 'soak' into the enemy, whereas, were you to draw apart, you would lose the chance to win. Research this well.

'TO INJURE THE CORNERS'

It is difficult to move strong things by pushing directly, so you should 'injure the corners'.

In large-scale strategy, it is beneficial to strike at the corners of the enemy's force. If the corners are overthrown, the spirit of the whole body will be overthrown. To defeat the enemy, you must follow up the attack when the corners have fallen.

In single combat, it is easy to win once the enemy collapses. This happens when you injure the 'corners' of his body, and this weakens him. It is important to know how to do this, so you must research it deeply.

TO THROW INTO CONFUSION

This means making the enemy lose resolve.

In large-scale strategy, we can use our troops to confuse the enemy on the field. Observing the enemy's spirit, we can make him think, 'Here? There? Like that? Like this? Slow? Fast?' Victory is certain when the enemy is caught up in a rhythm that confuses his spirit.

In single combat, we can confuse the enemy by attacking with varied techniques when the chance arises. Feint a thrust or cut, or make the enemy think you are going close to him, and when he is confused you can easily win.

This is the essence of fighting, and you must research it deeply.

THE THREE SHOUTS

The Three Shouts are divided thus: before, during and after. Shout according to the situation. The voice is a thing of life. We shout against fires and so on, against the wind and the waves. The voice shows energy.

In large-scale strategy, at the start of battle we shout as loudly as possible. During the fight, the voice is low-pitched, shouting out as we attack. After the contest, we shout in the wake of our victory. These are the Three Shouts.

In single combat, we make as if to cut and shout 'Ei!' at the same time to disturb the enemy, then in the wake of our shout we cut with the long sword. We shout after we have cut down the enemy – this is to announce victory. This is called 'sen go no koe' (before and after voice). We do not shout simultaneously with flourishing the long sword. We shout during the fight to get into rhythm. Research this deeply.

TO MINGLE

In battles, when the armies are in confrontation, attack the enemy's strong points and, when you see that they are beaten back, quickly separate and attack yet another strong point on the periphery of his force. The spirit of this is like a winding mountain path.

This is an important fighting method for one man against many. Strike down the enemies in one quarter, or drive them back, then grasp the timing and attack further strong points to right and left, as if on a winding mountain path, weighing up the enemies' disposition. When you know the enemies' level, attack strongly with no trace of retreating spirit.

In single combat, too, use this spirit with the enemy's strong points.

What is meant by 'mingling' is the spirit of advancing and becoming engaged with the enemy, and not withdrawing even one step. You must understand this.

TO CRUSH

This means to crush the enemy, regarding him as being weak.

In large-scale strategy, when we see that the enemy has few men, or if he has many men but his spirit is weak and disordered, we knock the hat over his eyes, crushing him utterly. If we crush lightly, he may recover. You must learn the spirit of crushing as if with a hand-grip.

In single combat, if the enemy is less skilful than yourself, if his rhythm is disorganized, or if he has fallen into evasive or retreating attitudes, we must crush him straightaway, with no concern for his presence and without allowing him space for breath. It is essential to crush him all at once. The primary thing is not to let him recover his position even a little. You must research this deeply.

THE 'MOUNTAIN–SEA CHANGE'

The 'mountain-sea' spirit means that it is bad to repeat the same thing several times when fighting the enemy. There may be no help but to do something twice, but do not try it a third time. If you once make an attack and fail, there is little chance of success if you use the same approach again. If you attempt a technique which you have previously tried unsuccessfully and fail yet again, then you must change your attacking method.

If the enemy thinks of the mountains, attack like the sea; and if he thinks of the sea, attack like the mountains. You must research this deeply.

'TO PENETRATE THE DEPTHS'

When we are fighting with the enemy, even when it can be seen that we can win on the surface with the benefit of the Way, if his spirit is not extinguished, he may be beaten superficially yet undefeated in spirit deep inside. With this principle of 'penetrating the depths' we can destroy the enemy's spirit in its depths, demoralizing him by quickly changing our spirit. This often occurs.

Penetrating the depths means penetrating with the long sword, penetrating with the body, and penetrating with the spirit. This cannot be understood in a generalization.

Once we have crushed the enemy in the depths, there is no need to remain spirited. But otherwise we must remain spirited. If the enemy remains spirited, it

is difficult to crush him. You must train in penetrating the depths for large-scale strategy and also single combat.

'TO RENEW'

'To renew' applies when we are fighting with the enemy, and an entangled spirit arises where there is no possible resolution. We must abandon our efforts, think of the situation in a fresh spirit, then win in the new rhythm. To renew, when we are deadlocked with the enemy, means that without changing our circumstance we change our spirit and win through a different technique.

It is necessary to consider how 'to renew' also applies in large-scale strategy. Research this diligently.

'RAT'S HEAD, OX'S NECK'

'Rat's head, ox's neck' means that, when we are fighting with the enemy and both he and we have become occupied with small points in an entangled spirit, we must always think of the Way of strategy as being both a rat's head and an ox's neck. Whenever we have become preoccupied with small details, we must suddenly change into a large spirit, interchanging large with small.

This is one of the essences of strategy. It is necessary that the warrior think in this spirit in everyday life. You must not depart from this spirit in large-scale strategy nor in single combat.

'THE COMMANDER KNOWS THE TROOPS'

'The commander knows the troops' applies everywhere in fights in my Way of strategy.

Using the wisdom of strategy, think of the enemy as your own troops. When you think in this way, you can move him at will and be able to chase him around. You become the general and the enemy becomes your troops. You must master this.

'TO LET GO THE HILT'

There are various kinds of spirit involved in letting go the hilt.

There is the spirit of winning without a sword. There is also the spirit of holding the long sword but not winning. The various methods cannot be expressed in writing. You must train well.

THE 'BODY OF A ROCK'[34]

When you have mastered the Way of strategy, you can suddenly make your body like a rock, and ten thousand things cannot touch you. This is the 'body of a rock'.

Oral tradition: You will not be moved.

What is recorded above is what has been constantly on my mind about Ichi school sword-fencing, written down as it came to me. This is the first time I have written about my technique, and the order of things is a bit confused. It is difficult to express it clearly.

This book is a spiritual guide for the man who wishes to learn the Way.

My heart has been inclined to the Way of strategy from my youth onwards. I have devoted myself to training my hand, tempering my body, and attaining the many spiritual attitudes of sword-fencing. If we watch men of other schools discussing theory, and concentrating on techniques with the hands, even though they seem skilful to watch, they have not the slightest true spirit.

Of course, men who study in this way think they are training the body and spirit, but it is an obstacle to the true Way, and its bad influence remains forever. Thus the true Way of strategy is becoming decadent and dying out.

The true Way of sword-fencing is the craft of defeating the enemy in a fight, and nothing other than this. If you attain and adhere to the wisdom of my strategy, you need never doubt that you will win.

The Wind Book

In strategy, you must know the Ways of other schools, so I have written
about various other traditions of strategy in this, the Wind Book.

Without knowledge of the Ways of other schools, it is difficult to understand the
essence of my Ichi school. Looking at other schools we find some that specialize
in techniques of strength using extra-long swords. Some schools study the Way
of the short sword, known as 'kodachi'. Some schools teach dexterity in large
numbers of sword techniques, teaching attitudes of the sword as the 'surface' and
the Way as the 'interior'.

That none of these are the true Way I show clearly in the interior of
this book – all the vices and virtues and rights and wrongs. My Ichi school
is different. Other schools make accomplishments their means of livelihood,
growing flowers and decoratively colouring articles in order to sell them. This is
definitely not the Way of strategy.

Some of the world's strategists are concerned only with sword-fencing, and
limit their training to flourishing the long sword and carriage of the body. But
is dexterity alone sufficient to win? This is not the essence of the Way.

I have recorded the unsatisfactory points of other schools one by one in this
book. You must study these matters deeply to appreciate the benefit of my Nito
Ichi school.

OTHER SCHOOLS USING EXTRA-LONG SWORDS

Some other schools have a liking for extra-long swords. From the point of view of my strategy, these must be seen as weak schools. This is because they do not appreciate the principle of cutting the enemy by any means. Their preference is for the extra-long sword and, relying on the virtue of its length, they think to defeat the enemy from a distance.

In this world it is said, 'One inch gives the hand advantage', but these are the idle words of one who does not know strategy. It shows the inferior strategy of a weak spirit that men should be dependent on the length of their sword, fighting from a distance without the benefit of strategy.

I expect there is a case for the school in question liking extra-long swords as part of its doctrine, but if we compare this with real life it is unreasonable. Surely, we need not necessarily be defeated if we are using a short sword and have no long sword?

It is difficult for these people to cut the enemy when at close quarters because of the length of the long sword. The blade path is large so the long sword is an encumbrance, and they are at a disadvantage compared to the man armed with a short companion sword.

From olden times it has been said: 'Great and small go together.' So do not unconditionally dislike extra-long swords. What I dislike is the inclination towards the long sword. If we consider large-scale strategy, we can think of large forces in terms of long swords, and small forces as short swords. Cannot few men give battle against many?

There are many instances of few men overcoming many.

Your strategy is of no account if, when called on to fight in a confined space, your heart is inclined to the long sword, or if you are in a house armed only with your companion sword. Besides, some men have not the strength of others.

In my doctrine, I dislike preconceived, narrow spirit. You must study this well.

THE STRONG LONG SWORD SPIRIT IN OTHER SCHOOLS

You should not speak of strong and weak long swords. If you just wield the long sword in a strong spirit your cutting will become coarse, and if you use the sword coarsely you will have difficulty in winning.

If you are concerned with the strength of your sword, you will try to cut unreasonably strongly, and will not be able to cut at all. It is also bad to try to cut strongly when testing the sword. Whenever you cross swords with an enemy you must not think of cutting him either strongly or weakly; just think of cutting and killing him. Be intent solely on killing the enemy. Do not try to cut strongly and, of course, do not think of cutting weakly. You should only be concerned with killing the enemy.

If you rely on strength, when you hit the enemy's sword you will inevitably hit too hard. If you do this, your own sword will be carried along as a result. Thus, the saying, 'The strongest hand wins', has no meaning.

In large-scale strategy, if you have a strong army and are relying on strength to win but the enemy also has a strong army, the battle will be fierce. This is the same for both sides.

Without the correct principle, the fight cannot be won.

The spirit of my school is to win through the wisdom of strategy, paying no attention to trifles. Study this well.

USE OF THE SHORTER LONG SWORD IN OTHER SCHOOLS

Using a shorter long sword is not the true Way to win.

In ancient times, 'tachi' and 'katana' meant long and short swords. Men of superior strength in the world can wield even a long sword lightly, so there is no case for their liking the short sword. They also make use of the length of spears and halberds. Some men use a shorter long sword with the intention of jumping in and stabbing the enemy at the unguarded moment when he flourishes his sword. This inclination is bad.

To aim for the enemy's unguarded moment is completely defensive, and undesirable at close quarters with the enemy. Furthermore, you cannot use the method of jumping inside his defence with a short sword if there are many enemies. Some men think that if they go against many enemies with a shorter long sword they can unrestrictedly frisk around cutting in sweeps, but they have to parry cuts continuously, and eventually become entangled with the enemy. This is inconsistent with the true Way of strategy.

The sure Way to win thus is to chase the enemy around in a confusing

manner, causing him to jump aside, with your body held strongly and straight. The same principle applies to large-scale strategy. The essence of strategy is to fall upon the enemy in large numbers and to bring about his speedy downfall. By their study of strategy, people of the world get used to countering, evading and retreating as the normal thing. They become set in this habit, so can easily be paraded around by the enemy. The Way of strategy is straight and true. You must chase the enemy around and make him obey your spirit.

OTHER SCHOOLS WITH MANY METHODS OF USING THE LONG SWORD

I think it is held in other schools that there are many ways of using the longsword in order to gain the admiration of beginners; this is selling the Way. It is a vile Spirit in strategy. The reason for this is that to deliberate over many ways of cutting down a man is an error.

To start with, killing is not the way of mankind. Killing is the same for women or children and there are not many methods. We can speak of tactics such as stabbing and mowing down but none other than these. Anyway, cutting down an enemy is the way of strategy and there is no need for many refinements of it.

Even so, according to the place obstructed above or to the sides and you will need to hold your sword in such a manner that it can be used. There are five methods in five directions. Methods apart from these five, hand twisting, body bending, jumping out and so on to cut the enemy are not the true way of strategy.

In order to cut the enemy you must not make twisting or bending cuts. This is completely useless. In my strategy I bear my spirit and body straight and cause the enemy to twist and bend.

The necessary Spirit is to win by attacking the enemy when his Spirit is warped. You must study this well.

USE OF ATTITUDES OF THE LONG SWORD IN OTHER SCHOOLS

Placing a great deal of importance on the attitudes of the long sword is a mistaken way of thinking. What is known in the world as 'attitude' applies when there is

no enemy. The reason is that this has been a precedent since ancient times, and there should be no such thing as 'This is the modern way to do it' in duelling. You must force the enemy into inconvenient situations.

Attitudes are for situations in which you are not to be moved. That is, for garrisoning castles, battle array, and so on, showing the spirit of not being moved even by a strong assault. In the Way of duelling, however, you must always be intent upon taking the lead and attacking. Attitude is the spirit of awaiting an attack. You must appreciate this.

In duels of strategy you must move the opponent's attitude. Attack where his spirit is lax, throw him into confusion, irritate and terrify him. Take advantage of the enemy's rhythm when he is unsettled and you can win.

I dislike the defensive spirit known as 'attitude'. Therefore, in my Way, there is something called 'Attitude-No-Attitude'.

In large-scale strategy, we deploy our troops for battle bearing in mind our strength, observing the enemy's numbers, and noting the details of the battlefield. This is at the start of the battle.

The spirit of attacking is completely different from the spirit of being attacked. Bearing an attack well, with a strong attitude, and parrying the enemy's attack well, is like making a wall of spears and halberds. When you attack the enemy, your spirit must go to the extent of pulling the stakes out of a wall and using them as spears and halberds. You must examine this well.

FIXING THE EYES IN OTHER SCHOOLS

Some schools maintain that the eyes should be fixed on the enemy's long sword. Some schools fix the eye on the hands. Some fix the eyes on the face, and some fix the eyes on the feet, and so on. If you fix the eyes on these places, your spirit can become confused and your strategy thwarted.

I will explain this in detail. Footballers[35] do not fix their eyes on the ball, but by good play on the field they can perform well. When you become accustomed to something, you are not limited to the use of your eyes. People such as master musicians have the music score in front of their nose, or flourish the sword in several ways when they have mastered the Way, but this does not mean they fix their eyes on these things specifically, or make pointless movements of the sword. It means they can see naturally.

In the Way of strategy, when you have fought many times you will easily be able to appraise the speed and position of the enemy's sword, and having mastery of the Way you will see the weight of his spirit. In strategy, fixing the eyes means gazing at the man's heart.

In large-scale strategy, the area to watch is the enemy's strength. 'Perception' and 'sight' are the two methods of seeing. Perception consists of concentrating strongly on the enemy's spirit, observing the condition of the battlefield, fixing the gaze strongly, seeing the progress of the fight and the changes of advantage. This is the sure way to win.

In single combat, you must not fix the eyes on details. As I said before, if you fix your eyes on details and neglect important things, your spirit will become bewildered, and victory will escape you. Research this principle well and train diligently.

USE OF THE FEET IN OTHER SCHOOLS

There are various methods of using the feet: floating foot, jumping foot, springing foot, treading foot, crow's foot, and such nimble walking methods. From the point of view of my strategy, these are all unsatisfactory.

I dislike floating foot because the feet always tend to float during the fight. The Way must be trod firmly.

Neither do I like jumping foot, because it encourages the habit of jumping, and a jumpy spirit. However much you jump, there is no real justification for it, so jumping is bad.

Springing foot causes a springing spirit which is indecisive.

Treading foot is a 'waiting' method, and I especially dislike it.

Apart from these, there are various fast walking methods, such as crow's foot, and so on.

Sometimes, however, you may encounter the enemy on marshland, swampy ground, river valleys, stony ground, or narrow roads, in which situations you cannot jump or move the feet quickly.

In my strategy, the footwork does not change. I always walk as I usually do in the street. You must never lose control of your feet. According to the enemy's rhythm, move fast or slowly, adjusting your body not too much and not too little.

Carrying the feet is important also in large-scale strategy. This is because, if you attack quickly and thoughtlessly without knowing the enemy's spirit, your rhythm will become deranged and you will not be able to win. Or, if you advance too slowly, you will not be able to take advantage of the enemy's disorder, the opportunity to win will escape, and you will not be able to finish the fight quickly. You must win by seizing upon the enemy's disorder and derangement, and by not according him even a little hope of recovery. Practise this well.

SPEED IN OTHER SCHOOLS

Speed is not part of the true Way of strategy. Speed implies that things seem fast or slow, according to whether or not they are in rhythm. Whatever the Way, the master of strategy does not appear fast.

Some people can walk as fast as a hundred or a hundred and twenty miles in a day, but this does not mean that they run continuously from morning till night. Unpractised runners may seem to have been running all day, but their performance is poor.

In the Way of dance, accomplished performers can sing while dancing, but when beginners try this they slow down and their spirit becomes busy. The 'old pine tree'[36] melody beaten on a leather drum is tranquil, but when beginners try this they slow down and their spirit becomes busy. Very skilful people can manage a fast rhythm, but it is bad to beat hurriedly. If you try to beat too quickly you will get out of time. Of course, slowness is bad. Really skilful people never get out of time, and are always deliberate, and never appear busy. From this example, the principle can be seen.

What is known as speed is especially bad in the Way of strategy. The reason for this is that depending on the place, marsh or swamp and so on, it may not be possible to move the body and legs together quickly. Still less will you be able to cut quickly if you have a long sword in this situation. If you try to cut quickly, as if using a fan or short sword, you will not actually cut even a little. You must appreciate this.

In large-scale strategy also, a fast, busy spirit is undesirable. The spirit must be that of 'holding down a pillow', then you will not be even a little late.

When your opponent is hurrying recklessly, you must act contrarily, and keep calm. You must not be influenced by the opponent. Train diligently to attain this spirit.

'INTERIOR' AND 'SURFACE' IN OTHER SCHOOLS

There is no 'interior' nor 'surface' in strategy.

The artistic accomplishments usually claim inner meaning and secret tradition, and 'interior' and 'gate'[37] but in combat there is no such thing as fighting on the surface, or cutting with the interior. When I teach my Way, I first teach by training in techniques which are easy for the pupil to understand, a doctrine which is easy to understand. I gradually endeavour to explain the deep principle, points which it is hardly possible to comprehend, according to the pupil's progress. In any event, because the way to understanding is through experience, I do not speak of 'interior' and 'gate'.

In this world, if you go into the mountains, and decide to go deeper and yet deeper, instead you will emerge at the gate. Whatever is the Way, it has an interior, and it is sometimes a good thing to point out the gate. In strategy, we cannot say what is concealed and what is revealed.

Accordingly, I dislike passing on my Way through written pledges and regulations. Perceiving the ability of my pupils, I teach the direct Way, remove the bad influence of other schools, and gradually introduce them to the true Way of the warrior.

The method of teaching my strategy is with a trustworthy spirit. You must train diligently.

I have tried to record an outline of the strategy of other schools in the above nine sections.

I could now continue by giving a specific account of these schools one by one, from the 'gate' to the 'interior', but I have intentionally not named the schools or their main points.

The reason for this is that different branches of schools give different interpretations of the doctrines. In as much as men's opinions differ, so there must be differing ideas on the same matter. Thus no one man's conception is valid for any school.

I have shown the general tendencies of other schools on nine points. If we look at them from an honest viewpoint, we see that people always tend to like long swords or short swords, and become concerned with strength in both large and small matters. You can see why I do not deal with the 'gates' of other schools.

In my Ichi school of the long sword there is neither gate nor interior. There is no inner meaning in sword attitudes. You must simply keep your spirit true to realize the virtue of strategy.

CHAPTER FIVE

The Book of the Void

The Nito Ichi Way of strategy is
recorded in this, the Book of the Void.
What is called the spirit of the void is where there is nothing.
It is not included in man's knowledge. Of course, the void
is nothingness. By knowing things that exist, you can
know that which does not exist. That is the void.

People in this world look at things mistakenly, and think that what they do not understand must be the void. This is not the true void. It is bewilderment.

In the Way of strategy, also, those who study as warriors think that whatever they cannot understand in their craft is the void. This is not the true void.

To attain the Way of strategy as a warrior, you must study fully other martial arts and not deviate even a little from the Way of the warrior. With your spirit settled, accumulate practice day by day, and hour by hour. Polish the twofold spirit, heart and mind, and sharpen the twofold gaze, perception and sight. When your spirit is not in the least clouded, when the clouds of bewilderment clear away, there is the true void.

Until you realize the true Way, whether in Buddhism or in common sense, you may think that things are correct and in order. However, if we look at things objectively, from the viewpoint of laws of the world, we see various doctrines departing from the true Way. Know well this spirit, and with forthrightness as

the foundation and the true spirit as the Way. Enact strategy broadly, correctly and openly.

Then you will come to think of things in a wide sense and, taking the void as the Way, you will see the Way as void.

In the void is virtue, and no evil. Wisdom has existence, principle has existence, the Way has existence, spirit is nothingness.

Endnotes

1   'Way' means the whole life of the warrior, his devotion to the sword, his place in the Confucius-coloured bureaucracy of the Tokugawa system. It is the road of the cosmos, not just a set of ethics for the artist or priest to live by, but the divine footprints of God pointing the Way.

2   Heaven means the Shinto religion. In Shinto there are many Holies, gods of steel and fermentation, place and industry and so on, and the first gods, ancestors to the Imperial line.

3   In Buddhism, Kwannon is the god(dess) of mercy.

4   Years, months and hours were named after the ancient Chinese zodiacal time system.

5   Waka is a 31-syllable poem. The word translates as 'song of Japan' or 'song in harmony'.

6   The bow was the main weapon of the samurai of the Nara and Heian periods, later superseded by the sword. Archery is practised as a ritual like tea and sword. Hachiman, the God of War, is often depicted as an archer, and the bow is frequently illustrated as part of the paraphernalia of the gods.

7   'Bunbu ichi' or 'Pen and sword in accord' is often presented in brushed calligraphy. Young men during the Tokugawa period were educated solely in writing the Chinese classics and exercising in swordplay. Pen and sword, in fact, filled the lives of the Japanese nobility.

8   This idea can be summed up as the philosophy expounded in *Hagakure* or Hidden Leaves, a book written in the seventeenth century by Yamamoto Tsunetomo and other samurai of the province Nabeshima Han, present-day Saga. Under the Tokugawas, the enforced logic of the Confucius-influenced system ensured stability among the samurai, but it also meant the passing of certain aspects of *Bushido*. Discipline for both samurai and commoners became lax. Yamamoto Tsunetomo had been counsellor to Mitsushige, lord of Nabeshima Han for many years, and upon his lord's death he wanted to commit suicide with his family in the traditional manner. But this was strictly prohibited by the new legislation and, full of remorse, Yamamoto retired in sadness to the boundary of Nabeshima Han. Here he met others who had faced the same predicament, and together they wrote a lament of what they saw as the decadence of *Bushido*. Their criticism is a revealing comment on the changing face of Japan during Musashi's lifetime: 'There is no way to describe what a warrior should do other than he should adhere to the Way of the warrior (*Bushido*). I find that all men are negligent of this. There are a few men who can quickly reply to the question, "What is the Way of the Warrior?" This is because they do not know in their hearts. From this we can say they do not follow the Way of the warrior. This means choosing death whenever there is a choice between life and death. It means nothing more than this. It means to see things through, being resolved. . . . If you keep your spirit correct from morning to night, accustomed to the idea of death and resolved on death, and consider yourself as a dead body, thus becoming one with the Way of the warrior, you can pass through life with no possibility of failure.

9   The original schools of Kendo can be found in the traditions preserved in Shinto shrines.

10 'Carpenter' means architect and builder. All buildings in Japan, except for the walls of the great castles which appeared a few generations before Musashi's birth, were made of wood.

11 'The Four Houses' refers to the four branches of the Fujiwara family who dominated Japan in the Heian period

12 Japanese buildings made liberal use of sliding doors, detachable walls, and shutters made of wood which were put over door openings at night and in bad weather.

13 Small shrines to the Shinto gods are found in every Japanese home.

14 The Five Greats of Buddhism are the elements that make up the cosmos: ground, water, fire, wind and void. The Five Rings of Buddhism are the five parts of the human body: head, left and right elbows, and left and right knees.

15 The Void, or Nothingness, is a Buddhist term for the illusory nature of worldly things.

16 The samurai wore two swords thrust through the belt, with the cutting edges upward on the left side. The shorter, or companion, sword was carried at all times and the longer sword worn only out of doors. From time to time there were rules governing the style and length of swords. While samurai carried two swords, other classes were allowed only one sword for protection against brigands on the roads between towns. The samurai kept their swords at their bedsides and there were racks for long swords inside the vestibule of every samurai home.

17 The techniques for spear and halberd fighting are the same as those of sword fighting. Spears were first popular in the Muromachi period, primarily as arms for the vast armies of common infantry, and later became objects of decoration for the processions of the *daimyō* to and from the capital in the Tokugawa period. The spear is used to cut and thrust, and is not thrown. The halberd and similar weapons with long curved blades were especially effective against cavalry, and came to be used by women who might have to defend their homes in the absence of menfolk.

18 The Japanese gun was the matchlock, which was first introduced into the country by missionaries and remained in common usage until the nineteenth century.

19 There are various kinds of dancing: festival dances, such as the harvest dance, which incorporate local characteristics and are very colourful, sometimes involving many people; and Noh theatre, which is enacted by a few performers using stylized dance movements. There are also dances of fan and dances of sword.

20 Dōjōs were mostly where a great deal of formality and ritual was observed, safe from the prying eyes of rival schools.

21 Swords were tested by highly specialized professional testers. The sword would be fitted into a special mounting and test cuts made on bodies, bundles of

straw, armour, sheets of metal and so on. Sometimes, appraisal marks of a sword testing inscribed on the tangs of old blades are found.

22 Different methods of moving are used in different schools. Yin–Yang, or 'In-Yo' in Japanese, is female–male, dark–light, right–left. Musashi advocates this 'level mind' kind of walking, although he is emphatic about the significance of these parameters. Issues of right and left foot arise in the Wind Book of *The Book of Five Rings*. Old Jujitsu schools advocate making the first attack with the left side forward.

23 The Way as a way of life, and as the natural path of a sword blade. There is a natural movement of the sword associated with a natural behaviour, according to Kendo ethics.

24 An item carried by men and women in the hot summer months. Armoured officers sometimes carried an iron war fan.

25 This means the ability to act calmly and naturally even in the face of danger. It is the highest accord with existence, when a man's word and his actions are spontaneously the same.

26 The lacquer work, which takes its name from Japan, was used to coat furniture and home utensils, architecture, weapons and armour.

27 Musashi is held to be the inventor of the two-sword style. His school is sometimes called 'Nito Ryu' ('two-sword school') and sometimes 'Niten Ryu' ('two heavens school'). He writes that the use of two swords is for when there are many enemies, but people practise a style of fencing with a sword in each hand to give practical advantage in fencing. Musashi used the words 'two swords' when meaning to use all one's resources in combat. He never used two swords when up against a skilled swordsman.

28 Other Kendo schools also have oral traditions as opposed to teachings passed on in formal technique.

29 There have been practice swords of various kinds throughout the history of Kendo – some are made of spliced bamboo covered with cloth or hide.

30 Cuirass, gauntlets, sleeves, apron and thigh pieces or, according to another convention, body armour, helmet, mask, thigh pieces, gauntlets and leg pieces.

31 The residence of the ancestral spirit of a house; the head of the house sits nearest this place. It is often a slightly raised recess in a wall, sometimes containing a hanging scroll, armour or other religious property.

32 A great swordsman or other artist will have mastered the ability to forestall the enemy. The great swordsman is always 'before' his environment. This does not mean speed. You cannot beat a good swordsman, because he subconsciously sees the origin of every real action. One can still see, in Kendo practice, wonderful old gentlemen slowly hitting young champions on the head almost casually. It is the practised ability to sum up a changing situation instantly.

33 The expression 'Yotsu te o hanasu' means the condition of grappling with both arms engaged with the opponent's arms. It is also the name used to describe various articles with four corners joined, such as a fishing net, and was given to an article of ladies' clothing which consisted of a square of cloth that tied from the back over each shoulder and under each arm, with a knot on the breast.

34 This is recorded in the *Terao Ka Ki*, the chronicle of the house of Terao. Once, a lord asked Musashi, 'What is this "body of a rock"?' Musashi replied, 'Please summon my pupil Terao Ryuma Suke.' When Terao appeared, Musashi ordered him to kill himself by cutting his abdomen. Just as Terao was about to make the cut, Musashi restrained him and said to the lord, 'This is the "body of a rock".'

35 Football was a court game in ancient Japan. There is a reference to it in a classic work of Japanese literature, *Genji Monogatari (The Tale of Genji)*.

36 'KoMatsu Bushi', an old tune for flute or lyre.

37 A student enrolling in a school would pass through the 'gate of the dōjō'. To enter a teacher's gate means to take up a course of study.

The Way of
the Samurai

Inazo Nitobe

Contents

Introduction

First published in 1900, Inazo Nitobe's classic exposition of the 'Way of the Samurai' was written at a time when Japan was undergoing a profound transformation as it emerged from the feudalism and 'closed doors' seclusion of the Edo Period to become a modern nation. Originally written in English for Western readers and published under the title *Bushido: The Soul of Japan*, the present book was one of the first major works to offer an insightful account of the principles underlying the samurai tradition and the influential role these had played in the moulding of Japanese culture and the character of the Japanese people, both of which appeared alien to contemporary Western eyes. As such it was read by many influential foreigners, among whom may be counted President Theodore Roosevelt, President John F. Kennedy and Robert Baden-Powell, founder of the Boy Scout movement, who is said to have studied the educational techniques of *bushido* while writing *Scouting For Boys*.

Following its original publication in English, Nitobe's book was subsequently translated into Japanese and many other languages and was influential in bringing the word 'Bushido' (meaning 'the way of the samurai') into common usage. The principles/ideals now widely known as Bushido had already begun to evolve by the 8th century AD, when the term *bushi* was used to refer to the educated warrior-poet ideal that later became synonymous with the samurai. This ancient ideal of the warrior-poet was encapsulated in the pictogram for the word

uruwashii (an early term for samurai) which combined the characters for *bun* (literary study) and *bu* (military arts), whereas early usage of the word *samurai* (meaning 'those who serve in close attendance to the nobility') was reserved for a particular class or rank of public servant – it did not become associated with military men until several centuries later. A distinct aristocratic military class came into being in the late 12th century during the Kamakura Shogunate and evolved over subsequent centuries to fulfil the ideal expressed in the ancient saying *Bun Bu Ryo Do* – 'literary arts and military arts in equal measure.' Over time this aristocratic warrior or samurai class developed a distinctive culture of its own, which in turn influenced Japanese culture as a whole – the tea ceremony, monochrome ink painting, rock gardens and poetry were all inherited from the samurai. During the Edo or Tokugawa Period (1603–1868), Japan experienced a period of relative peace after centuries of clan wars, and it was during this peaceful period that the principles/ideals of Bushido were further refined by the aristocratic samurai class.

Inazo Nitobe's own samurai heritage dates back to the late 12th century and the dawn of the Kamakura Era when, in keeping with feudal tradition, Yoritamo Minamoto awarded a new fief to Tsunehide Chiba for services rendered in battle. Chiba moved his family to Nitobe, which was part of his new domain, and five generations later the family changed its surname from Chiba to Nitobe. Subsequent defeats in battle and loss of land saw the Nitobes move to northern Japan at the beginning of the Edo Period, where they became vassals of the Nanbu family. In the 19th century, Koretami Nitobe (Inazo's great-grandfather) wrote several works on Uesugi military strategy, while Inazo's grandfather (Tsuto) and father (Jujiro) began work on the Inaoigawa irrigation canal which turned the previously barren region around present-day Towada into a productive rice-growing area – when the first rice plants (*ine*) appeared, the family celebrated by naming its newest addition 'Inenosuke' (later shortened to Inazo).

BUSHIDO: THE WAY OF THE SAMURAI

As already mentioned, the present book was written at a time when Japan had only recently emerged from a prolonged period of feudalism. This had much in common with the feudalism of medieval Europe and Nitobe draws on their similarities to present the samurai as being, in many ways, the Japanese equivalent of the European knight or *chevalier*. But for Nitobe such references to the similarities between European and Japanese culture have an underlying purpose which he explains in his preface: 'All through the discourse I have tried to illustrate whatever points I have made with parallel examples from European history and literature, believing that these will aid in bringing the subject nearer the comprehension of foreign readers.' Having been born to a samurai family when feudalism was still in force, and having studied at universities in both Europe and the USA, Nitobe was uniquely qualified to make such parallel examples.

Nitobe defines Bushido as 'the code of moral principles' which the samurai 'were required or instructed to observe. It is not a written code... It was an organic growth of decades and centuries of military career.' In the course of this organic growth Bushido was influenced by a variety of sources, assimilating readily those that coincided closest with the innate character of the Japanese. A quick glance at the principal sources of Bushido outlined by Nitobe in Chapter 2 – Shintoism, Buddhism, Zen and the teachings of the Chinese philosophers Confucius and Mencius – suggests that the Way of the Samurai incorporated a strong spiritual element. Further evidence for this is to be found in the chapters dedicated to the moral qualities that moulded the character of the samurai – rectitude or justice, courage, benevolence, politeness, veracity or sincerity, honour, loyalty and self-control – for the genuine attainment of these qualities necessitates a diminution of the ego similar to that advocated by any spiritual path. By vowing to loyally serve his lord even if it meant losing his own life, the samurai freed himself from motives of self-interest or self-aggrandisement. The qualities listed above also served to mould the national character of the Japanese, especially in the emphasis based on customs of politeness, which could be somewhat perplexing for the many foreigners visiting Japan for the first time. In Chapter 6, Nitobe tells of the occasion when someone remarked that certain Japanese customs were 'awfully funny.' His ensuing explanation of the motivation behind several 'awfully funny' customs is enlightening as is his explanation in the same chapter of the spiritual significance of *Cha-no-yu* (the tea ceremony).

There were also certain Japanese customs that appeared to be far from funny to Western eyes, the principal one being the practice of *seppuku* (better known as *hara-kiri*), which means 'self-immolation by disembowelment.' In Chapter 12, Nitobe explains that '*seppuku* was not a mere suicide process. It was an institution, legal and ceremonial.' *Seppuku* was obsolete by the time Nitobe wrote his book but he includes a lengthy eye-witness account of one such ceremony. Chapter 14 on the training and position of women in the samurai class may appear equally disturbing. Nitobe was aware that to Western eyes it would appear that samurai women were treated as inferior to men, but he explains that this was not the case – a woman was not 'the slave of man,' her role was 'recognised as *naijo*, "the inner-help".'

In the final chapter, Nitobe ponders the future of Bushido and draws the following conclusion:

> Bushido as an independent code of ethics may vanish, but its power will not perish from the face of the earth; its schools of martial prowess or civic honour may be demolished, but its light and its glory will long survive their ruins.

INAZO NITOBE (1862–1933)

A distinguished agricultural economist, author, educator, diplomat and statesman, Inazo Nitobe was born in Morioka, in what is now the Iwate Prefecture. His father, Jujiro Nitobe, died when Inazo was only five years old and in 1869 he moved to Tokyo to live with his adoptive uncle, Tokitoshi Ota, to whom he dedicated the present book because he had taught him at an early age 'to revere the past and to admire the deeds of the samurai.' In 1877 Inazo entered the Sapporo Agricultural College (now Hokkaido University) to study agriculture, a decision that was probably due to Emperor Meiji's wish that the Nitobe family continue with their development of the once-barren land near present-day Towada. Sapporo had been founded the preceding year by William S. Clark, former President of the Massachusetts Agricultural College, and Clark's influence was such that some 30 or so students, including Inazo Nitobe, converted to Christianity.

In 1883, Nitobe began studying English literature and economics at Tokyo University but left within a year to continue his studies in the United States, at Johns Hopkins University in Baltimore. While there he became a member of the Religious Society of Friends (Quakers), through whom he met his future wife, Mary Patterson Elkinton. From Baltimore he went to Halle University in Germany, where he gained a doctorate in agricultural economics, and then returned briefly to Philadelphia to marry Mary Elkinton before taking up an assistant professorship at Sapporo in 1891. Appointments to full professorships followed – first at Kyoto Imperial University and then at the Law Faculty at Tokyo Imperial University – and in 1918 he was appointed founding president of Tokyo Joshi Dai (Tokyo Women's University).

In 1919 Nitobe attended the Paris Peace Conference and in the aftermath of World War I joined with other reform-minded Japanese in setting up the Japan Council of the Institute of Pacific Relations. In 1920 he moved to Geneva, Switzerland, to become one of the Under-Secretaries General of the newly established League of Nations. He also became a founding director of the International Committee on Intellectual Cooperation (the precursor of UNESCO). On his retirement from the League of Nations he returned to Japan and served in the House of Peers in the Japanese Imperial Parliament where he spoke out against the increasing militarism of Japan. In 1933, he attended a conference of the Institute of Pacific Relations in Banff, Alberta. On his way home from the conference he succumbed to pneumonia and died in hospital in Victoria, British Columbia, at the age of 71.

The present book is perhaps the best known of Nitobe's written works, but he was such a prolific author that the Japanese edition of his complete works extends to 25 volumes while his works in English and other Western languages have been published as a five-volume set. His life-long goal to become 'a bridge across the Pacific' is celebrated in several biographies in both English and Japanese and in two memorial gardens in Canada – one at the Royal Jubilee Hospital in Victoria, British Columbia, the other at the University of British Columbia Botanical Garden and Centre for Plant Research in Vancouver. With its Tea House and Stroll Garden, the latter is considered to be one of the most authentic Japanese gardens in North America and one of the finest outside of

Japan. The Nitobe Memorial Museum in Towada City, Japan, celebrates the life of Inazo Nitobe as well as the lives of his father and grandfather, whose irrigation canals brought new life to the region. The museum's tribute to the Nitobe family's long samurai history includes a collection of armour and other military artefacts. Inazo Nitobe recently received recognition of a different kind when his portrait was featured on the ¥5,000 note from 1984 to 2004.

> *What is important is to try to develop insights and wisdom rather than mere knowledge, respect someone's character rather than his learning, and nurture men of character rather than mere talents.*

Inazo Nitobe

John Baldock

Dedication

TO MY BELOVED UNCLE TOKITOSHI OTA
WHO TAUGHT ME TO REVERE THE PAST
AND TO ADMIRE THE DEEDS OF THE SAMURAI
I DEDICATE THIS LITTLE BOOK

'There are, if I may so say, three powerful spirits, which have from time to time, moved on the face of the waters, and given a predominant impulse to the moral sentiments and energies of mankind. These are the spirits of liberty, of religion, and of honour.'

Hallam, *Europe in the Middle Ages*

'Chivalry is itself the poetry of life.'

Schlegel, *Philosophy of History*

Preface

About ten years ago, while spending a few days under the hospitable roof of the distinguished Belgian jurist, the lamented M. de Laveleye, our conversation turned, during one of our rambles, to the subject of religion. 'Do you mean to say,' asked the venerable professor, 'that you have no religious instruction in your schools?' On my replying in the negative he suddenly halted in astonishment, and in a voice which I shall not easily forget, he repeated 'No religion! How do you impart moral education?' The question stunned me at the time. I could give no ready answer, for the moral precepts I learned in my childhood days were not given in schools; and not until I began to analyze the different elements that formed my notions of right and wrong, did I find that it was Bushido[1] that breathed them into my nostrils.

The direct inception of this little book is due to the frequent queries put by my wife as to the reasons why such and such ideas and customs prevail in Japan.

In my attempts to give satisfactory replies to M. de Laveleye and to my wife, I found that without understanding Feudalism and Bushido, the moral ideas of present Japan are a sealed volume.

Taking advantage of enforced idleness on account of long illness, I put down in the order now presented to the public some of the answers given in our household conversation. They consist mainly of what I was taught and told in my youthful days, when Feudalism was still in force.

Between Lafcadio Hearn and Mrs. Hugh Fraser on one side and Sir Ernest Satow and Professor Chamberlain on the other, it is indeed discouraging to write anything Japanese in English. The only advantage I have over them is that I can assume the attitude of a personal defendant, while these distinguished writers are at best solicitors and attorneys. I have often thought, 'Had I their gift of language, I would present the cause of Japan in more eloquent terms!' But one who speaks in a borrowed tongue should be thankful if he can just make himself intelligible.

All through the discourse I have tried to illustrate whatever points I have made with parallel examples from European history and literature, believing that these will aid in bringing the subject nearer to the comprehension of foreign readers.

Should any of my allusions to religious subjects and to religious workers be thought slighting, I trust my attitude towards Christianity itself will not be questioned. It is with ecclesiastical methods and with the forms which obscure the teachings of Christ, and not with the teachings themselves, that I have little sympathy. I believe in the religion taught by Him and handed down to us in the New Testament, as well as in the law written in the heart. Further, I believe that God hath made a testament which may be called 'old' with every people and nation – Gentile or Jew, Christian or Heathen. As to the rest of my theology, I need not impose upon the patience of the public.

In concluding this preface, I wish to express my thanks to my friend Anna C. Hartshorne for many valuable suggestions.

Inazo Nitobe

CHAPTER ONE

Bushido as an Ethical System

Chivalry is a flower no less indigenous to the soil of Japan than its emblem, the cherry blossom; nor is it a dried-up specimen of an antique virtue preserved in the herbarium of our history. It is still a living object of power and beauty among us; and if it assumes no tangible shape or form, it not the less scents the moral atmosphere, and makes us aware that we are still under its potent spell. The conditions of society which brought it forth and nourished it have long disappeared; but as those far-off stars which once were and are not, still continue to shed their rays upon us, so the light of chivalry, which was a child of feudalism, still illuminates our moral path, surviving its mother institution. It is a pleasure to me to reflect upon this subject in the language of Burke, who uttered the well-known touching eulogy over the neglected bier of its European prototype.

It argues a sad defect of information concerning the Far East, when so erudite a scholar as Dr. George Miller did not hesitate to affirm that chivalry, or any other similar institution, has never existed either among the nations of antiquity or among the modern Orientals[2]. Such ignorance, however, is amply excusable, as the third edition of the good Doctor's work appeared the same year that Commodore Perry was knocking at the portals of our exclusivism. More than a decade later, about the time that our feudalism was in the last throes of existence, Karl Marx, writing his *Capital*, called the attention of his readers to the peculiar advantage of studying the social and political institutions of feudalism, as then to be seen in living form only in Japan. I would likewise invite the Western historical and ethical student to the study of chivalry in the Japan of the present.

Enticing as is a historical disquisition on the comparison between European and Japanese feudalism and chivalry, it is not the purpose of this paper to enter into it at length. My attempt is rather to relate, *firstly*, the origin and sources of our chivalry; *secondly*, its character and teaching; *thirdly*, its influence among the masses; and, *fourthly*, the continuity and permanence of its influence. Of these several points, the first will be only brief and cursory, or else I should have to take my readers into the devious paths of our national history; the second will be dwelt upon at greater length, as being most likely to interest students of International Ethics and Comparative Ethology in our ways of thought and action; and the rest will be dealt with as corollaries.

The Japanese word which I have roughly rendered Chivalry, is, in the original, more expressive than Horsemanship. *Bu-shi-do* means literally Military–Knight–Ways – the ways which fighting nobles should observe in their daily life as well as in their vocation; in a word, the 'Precepts of Knighthood,' the *noblesse oblige* of the warrior class. Having thus given its literal significance, I may be allowed henceforth to use the word in the original. The use of the original term

is also advisable for this reason, that a teaching so circumscribed and unique, engendering a cast of mind and character so peculiar, so local, must wear the badge of its singularity on its face; then, some words have a national *timbre* so expressive of race characteristics that the best of translators can do them but scant justice, not to say positive injustice, and grievance. Who can improve by translation what the German *Gemüth* signifies, or who does not feel the difference between the two words verbally so closely allied as the English *gentleman* and the French *gentilhomme*?

Bushido, then, is the code of moral principles which the knights were required or instructed to observe. It is not a written code; at best it consists of a few maxims handed down from mouth to mouth or coming from the pen of some well-known warrior or savant. More frequently it is a code unuttered and unwritten, possessing all the more the powerful sanction of veritable deed, and of a law written on the fleshly tablets of the heart. It was founded not on the creation of one brain, however able, or on the life of a single personage, however renowned. It was an organic growth of decades and centuries of military career. It, perhaps, fills the same position in the history of ethics that the English Constitution does in political history; yet it has had nothing to compare with the Magna Carta or the Habeas Corpus Act. True, early in the

seventeenth century Military Statutes (*Buké Hatto*) were promulgated; but their thirteen short articles were taken up mostly with marriages, castles, leagues, etc., and didactic regulations were but meagrely touched upon. We cannot, therefore, point out any definite time and place and say, 'Here is its fountain head.' Only as it attains consciousness in the feudal age, its origin, in respect to time, may be identified with feudalism. But feudalism itself is woven of many threads, and Bushido shares its intricate nature. As in England the political institutions of feudalism may be said to date from the Norman Conquest, so we may say that in Japan its rise was simultaneous with the ascendancy of Yoritomo, late in the twelfth century. As, however, in England, we find the social elements of feudalism far back in the period previous to William the Conqueror, so, too, the germs of feudalism in Japan had been long existent before the period I have mentioned.

Again, in Japan as in Europe, when feudalism was formally inaugurated, the professional class of warriors naturally came into prominence. These were known as *samurai*, meaning literally, like the old English *cniht* (knecht, knight), guards or attendants – resembling in character the *soldurii* whom Caesar mentioned as existing in Aquitania, or the *comitati*, who, according to Tacitus, followed Germanic chiefs in his time; or, to take a still later parallel, the *milites medii* that one reads about in the history of Medieval Europe. A Sinico-Japanese word *Bu-ké* or *Bu-shi* (Fighting Knights) was also adopted in common use. They were a privileged class, and must originally have been a rough breed who made fighting their vocation. This class was naturally recruited, in a long period of constant warfare, from the manliest and the most adventurous, and all the while the process of elimination went on, the timid and the feeble being sorted out, and only 'a rude race, all masculine, with brutish strength,' to borrow Emerson's phrase, surviving to form families and the ranks of the *samurai*. Coming to profess great honour and great privileges, and correspondingly great responsibilities, they soon felt the need of a common standard of behaviour, especially as they were always on a belligerent footing and belonged to different clans. Just as physicians limit competition among themselves by professional courtesy, just as lawyers sit in courts of honour in cases of violated etiquette, so must also warriors possess some resort for final judgment on their misdemeanours.

Fair play in fight! What fertile germs of morality lie in this primitive sense of savagery and childhood. Is it not the root of all military and civic virtues? We smile (as if we had outgrown it!) at the boyish desire of the small Britisher, Tom Brown, 'to leave behind him the name of a fellow who never bullied a little boy or turned his back on a big one.' And yet, who does not know that this desire is the cornerstone on which moral structures of mighty dimensions can be reared? May I not go even so far as to say that the gentlest and most peace-loving of religions endorses this aspiration? This desire of Tom's is the basis on which the greatness of England is largely built, and it will not take us long to discover that Bushido does not stand on a lesser pedestal. If fighting in itself, be it offensive or defensive, is, as Quakers rightly testify, brutal and wrong, we can still say with Lessing, 'We know from what failings our virtue springs.' 'Sneaks' and 'cowards' are epithets of the worst opprobrium to healthy, simple natures. Childhood begins life with these notions, and knighthood also; but, as life grows larger and its relations many-sided, the early faith seeks sanction from higher authority and more rational sources for its own justification, satisfaction and development. If military interests had operated alone, without higher moral support, how far short of chivalry would the ideal of knighthood have fallen! In Europe, Christianity, interpreted with concessions convenient to chivalry, infused it nevertheless with spiritual data. 'Religion, war and glory were the three souls of a perfect Christian knight,' says Lamartine. In Japan there were several sources of Bushido.

CHAPTER TWO

Sources of Bushido

I may begin with Buddhism. It furnished a sense of calm trust in Fate, a quiet submission to the inevitable, that stoic composure in sight of danger or calamity, that disdain of life and friendliness with death. A foremost teacher of swordsmanship, when he saw his pupil master the utmost of his art, told him, 'Beyond this my instruction must give way to Zen teaching.' 'Zen' is the Japanese equivalent for the Dhyâna, which 'represents human effort to reach through meditation zones of thought beyond the range of verbal expression.'[3] Its method is contemplation, and its purport, as far as I understand it, to be convinced of a principle that underlies all phenomena, and, if it can, of the Absolute itself, and thus to put oneself in harmony with this Absolute. Thus defined, the teaching was more than the dogma of a sect, and whoever attains to the perception of the Absolute raises himself above mundane things and awakes, 'to a new Heaven and a new Earth.'

What Buddhism failed to give, Shintoism offered in abundance. Such loyalty to the sovereign, such reverence for ancestral memory, and such filial piety as are not taught by any other creed, were inculcated by the Shinto doctrines, imparting passivity to the otherwise arrogant character of the samurai. Shinto theology has no place for the dogma of 'original sin.' On the contrary, it believes in the innate goodness and God-like purity of the human soul, adoring it as the adytum from which divine oracles are proclaimed. Everybody has observed that the Shinto shrines are conspicuously devoid of objects and instruments of worship, and that a plain mirror hung in the sanctuary forms the essential part of its furnishing. The presence of this article is easy to explain: it typifies the human heart, which, when perfectly placid and clear, reflects the very image of the Deity. When you stand, therefore, in front of the shrine to worship, you see your own image reflected on its shining surface, and the act of worship is tantamount to the old Delphic injunction, 'Know Thyself.' But self-knowledge does not imply, either in the Greek or Japanese teaching, knowledge of the physical part of man, not his anatomy or his psycho-physics; knowledge was to be of a moral kind, the introspection of our moral nature. Mommsen, comparing the Greek and the Roman, says that when the former worshipped he raised his eyes to heaven, for his prayer was contemplation, while the latter veiled his head, for his was reflection. Essentially like the Roman conception of religion, our reflection brought into prominence not so much the moral as the national consciousness of the individual. Its nature-worship endeared the country to our inmost souls, while its ancestor-worship, tracing from lineage to lineage, made the Imperial family the fountain-head of the whole nation. To us the country is more than land and soil from which to mine gold or to reap grain – it is the sacred abode of the gods, the spirits of our forefathers: to us the Emperor is more than the Arch Constable of a *Rechtsstaat*, or even the Patron of a *Culturstaat* – he is the bodily representative of Heaven on earth, blending in his person its power and its mercy. If what M. Boutmy[4] says is true of English royalty – that it 'is not only the image of authority, but the author and symbol of national unity,' as I believe it to be, doubly and trebly may this be affirmed of royalty in Japan.

The tenets of Shintoism cover the two predominating features of the emotional life of our race – Patriotism and Loyalty. Arthur May Knapp very truly says: 'In Hebrew literature it is often difficult to tell whether the writer is speaking of God or of the Commonwealth; of heaven or of Jerusalem; of the Messiah or of the nation itself.'[5] A similar confusion may be noticed in the nomenclature of our national faith. I said confusion, because it will be so deemed by a logical intellect on account of its verbal ambiguity; still, being a framework of national instinct and race feelings, Shintoism never pretends to a systematic philosophy or a rational theology. This religion – or, is it not more correct to say, the race emotions which this religion expressed? – thoroughly imbued Bushido with loyalty to the sovereign and love of country. These acted more as impulses than as doctrines; for Shintoism, unlike the Medieval Christian Church, prescribed to its votaries scarcely any *credenda*, furnishing them at the same time with *agenda* of a straightforward and simple type.

As to strictly ethical doctrines, the teachings of Confucius were the most prolific source of Bushido. His enunciation of the five moral relations between master and servant (the governing and the governed), father and son, husband and wife, older and younger brother, and between friend and friend, was but a

confirmation of what the race instinct had recognized before his writings were introduced from China. The calm, benignant, and worldly-wise character of his politico-ethical precepts was particularly well suited to the samurai, who formed the ruling class. His aristocratic and conservative tone was well adapted to the requirements of these warrior statesmen. Next to Confucius, Mencius exercised an immense authority over Bushido. His forcible and often quite democratic theories were exceedingly taking to sympathetic natures, and they were even thought dangerous to, and subversive of, the existing social order, hence his works were for a long time under censure. Still, the words of this mastermind found permanent lodgment in the heart of the samurai.

The writings of Confucius and Mencius formed the principal text-books for youths and the highest authority in discussion among the old. A mere acquaintance with the classics of these two sages was held, however, in no high esteem. A common proverb ridicules one who has only an intellectual knowledge of Confucius, as a man ever studious but ignorant of *Analects*. A typical samurai calls a literary savant a book-smelling sot. Another compares learning to an ill-smelling vegetable that must be boiled and boiled before it is fit for use. A man who has read a little smells a little pedantic, and a man who has read much smells yet more so; both are alike unpleasant. The writer meant thereby that knowledge becomes really such only when it is assimilated in the mind of the learner and shows in his character.

Bushido made light of knowledge as such. It was not pursued as an end in itself, but as a means to the attainment of wisdom. Hence, he who stopped short of this end was regarded no higher than a convenient machine, which could turn out poems and maxims at bidding. Thus, knowledge was conceived as identical with its practical application in life; and this Socratic doctrine found its greatest exponent in the Chinese philosopher, Wan Yang Ming, who never wearies of repeating, 'To know and to act are one and the same.'

I beg leave for a moment's digression while I am on this subject, inasmuch as some of the noblest types of *bushi* were strongly influenced by the teachings of this sage. Western readers will easily recognize in his writings many parallels to the New Testament. Making allowance for the terms peculiar to either teaching, the passage, 'Seek ye first the kingdom of God and his righteousness; and all these things shall be added unto you,' conveys a thought that may be found on almost any page of Wan Yang Ming. A Japanese disciple[6] of his says – 'The lord of heaven and earth, of all living beings, dwelling in the heart of man, becomes his mind (*Kokoro*); hence a mind is a living thing, and is ever luminous': and again, 'The spiritual light of our essential being is pure, and is not affected by the will of man. Spontaneously springing up in our mind, it shows what is right and wrong: it is then called conscience; it is even the light that proceedeth from the god of heaven.' How very much do these words sound like some passages from Isaac Pennington or other philosophic mystics! I am inclined to think that the Japanese mind, as expressed in the simple tenets of the Shinto religion, was particularly open to the reception of Yang Ming's precepts. He carried his doctrine of the infallibility of conscience to extreme transcendentalism, attributing to it the faculty to perceive, not only the distinction between right and wrong, but also the nature of psychical facts and physical phenomena.

Thus, whatever the sources, the essential principles which Bushido imbibed from them and assimilated to itself, were few and simple. Few and simple as these were, they were sufficient to furnish a safe conduct of life even through the unsafest days of the most unsettled period of our nation's history. The wholesome, unsophisticated nature of our warrior ancestors derived ample food for their spirit from a sheaf of commonplace and fragmentary teachings, gleaned as it were on the highways and byways of ancient thought, and, stimulated by the demands of the age, formed from these gleanings a new and unique type of manhood. An acute French *savant*, M. de la Mazelière, thus sums up his impressions of the sixteenth century: 'Toward the middle of the sixteenth century, all is confusion in Japan, in the government, in society, in the church. But the civil wars, the manners returning to barbarism, the necessity for each to execute justice for himself – these formed men comparable to those Italians of the sixteenth century, in whom Taine praises "the vigorous initiative, the habit of sudden resolutions and desperate undertakings, the grand capacity to do and to suffer." In Japan as in Italy "the rude manners of the Middle Ages" made of man a superb animal, "wholly militant and wholly resistant." And this is why the sixteenth century displays in the highest degree the principal quality of the Japanese race, that great diversity which one finds there between minds (*esprits*) as well as between temperaments. While in India and even in China men seem to differ chiefly in degree of energy or intelligence, in Japan they differ by originality of character as well.'

To the pervading characteristics of the men of whom M. de la Mazelière writes, let us now address ourselves. I shall begin with Rectitude.

CHAPTER THREE

Rectitude or Justice

Here we discern the most cogent precept in the code of the samurai. Nothing is more loathsome to him than underhand dealings and crooked undertakings. The conception of Rectitude may be erroneous – it may be narrow. A well-known bushi defines it as a power of resolution; 'Rectitude is the power of deciding upon a certain course of conduct in accordance with reason, without wavering – to die when it is right to die, to strike when to strike is right.' Another speaks of it in the following terms: 'Rectitude is the bone that gives firmness and stature. As without bones the head cannot rest on the top of the spine, nor hands move nor feet stand, so without rectitude neither talent nor learning can make of a human frame a samurai. With it the lack of accomplishments is as nothing.' Mencius calls Benevolence man's mind, and Rectitude or Righteousness his path. 'How lamentable,' he exclaims, 'is it to neglect the path and not pursue it, to lose the mind and not know to seek it again! When men's fowls and dogs are lost, they know to seek for them again, but they lose their mind and do not know to seek for it.' Righteousness, according to Mencius, is a straight and narrow path which a man ought to take to regain the lost paradise.

Even in the latter days of feudalism, when the long continuance of peace brought leisure into the life of the warrior class, and with it dissipations of all kinds and gentle accomplishments, the epithet *Gishi* (a man of rectitude) was considered superior to any name that signified mastery of learning or art. The

Forty-seven Faithfuls – of whom so much is made in our popular education – are known in common parlance as the Forty-seven *Gishi*.

In times when cunning artifice was liable to pass for military tact and downright falsehood for *ruse de guerre*, this manly virtue, frank and honest, was a jewel that shone the brightest and was most highly praised. Rectitude is a twin brother to Valour, another martial virtue. But before proceeding to speak of Valour, let me linger a little while on what I may term a derivation from Rectitude, which, at first deviating slightly from its original, became more and more removed from it, until its meaning was perverted in the popular acceptance. I speak of *Gi-ri*, literally the Right Reason, but which came in time to mean a vague sense of duty which public opinion expected an incumbent to fulfil. In its original and unalloyed sense, it meant duty, pure and simple – hence, we speak of the *Giri* we owe to parents, to superiors, to inferiors, to society at large, and so forth. In these instances *Giri* is duty; for what else is duty than what Right Reason demands and commands us to do. Should not Right Reason be our categorical imperative?

Giri primarily meant no more than duty, and I dare say its etymology was derived from the fact that in our conduct, say to our parents, though love should be the only motive, lacking that, there must be some other authority to enforce filial piety; and they formulated this authority in *Giri*. Very rightly did they formulate this authority – *Giri* – since if love does not rush to deeds of virtue, recourse must be had to man's intellect and his reason must be quickened to convince him of the necessity of acting aright. The same is true of any other moral obligation. The instant Duty becomes onerous, Right Reason steps in to prevent our shirking it. *Giri* thus understood is a severe taskmaster, with a birch-rod in his hand to make sluggards perform their part. It is a secondary power in ethics; as a motive it is infinitely inferior to the Christian doctrine of love, which should be *the* law. I deem it a product of the conditions of an artificial society – of a society in which accident of birth and unmerited favour instituted class distinctions, in which the family was the social unit, in which seniority of age was of more account than superiority of talents, in which natural affections had often to succumb before arbitrary man-made customs. Because of this very artificiality, *Giri* in time degenerated into a vague sense of propriety called up to explain this and sanction that — as, for example, why a mother must, if need be, sacrifice all her other children in order to save the first-born; or why a daughter must sell her chastity to get funds to pay for the father's dissipation, and the like. Starting as Right Reason, *Giri* has, in my opinion, often stooped to casuistry. It has even degenerated into cowardly fear of censure. I might say of *Giri* what Scott wrote of patriotism, that 'as it is the fairest, so it is often the most suspicious, mask of other feelings.' Carried beyond or below Right Reason, *Giri* became a monstrous misnomer. It harboured under its wings every sort of sophistry and hypocrisy. It might easily have been turned into a nest of cowardice, if Bushido had not a keen and correct sense of courage, the spirit of daring and bearing.

CHAPTER FOUR

Courage, the Spirit
of Daring and Bearing

Courage was scarcely deemed worthy to be counted among virtues, unless it was exercised in the cause of Righteousness. In his *Analects* Confucius defines Courage by explaining, as is often his wont, what its negative is. 'Perceiving what is right,' he says, 'and doing it not, argues lack of courage.' Put this epigram into a positive statement, and it runs, 'Courage is doing what is right.' To run all kinds of hazards, to jeopardize one's self, to rush into the jaws of death – these are too often identified with Valour, and in the profession of arms such rashness of conduct – what Shakespeare calls, 'valour misbegot' – is unjustly applauded; but not so in the Precepts of Knighthood. Death for a cause unworthy of dying for, was called a 'dog's death.' 'To rush into the thick of battle and to be slain in it,' says a Prince of Mito, 'is easy enough, and the merest churl is equal to the task; but,' he continues, 'it is true courage to live when it is right to live, and to die only when it is right to die,' and yet the Prince had not even heard of the name of Plato, who defines courage as 'the knowledge of things that a man should fear and that he should not fear.' A distinction which is made in the West between moral and physical courage has long been recognized among us. What samurai youth has not heard of 'Great Valour' and the 'Valour of a Villain'?

Valour, Fortitude, Bravery, Fearlessness, Courage, being the qualities of soul which appeal most easily to juvenile minds, and which can be trained by exercise and example, were, so to speak, the most popular virtues, early emulated among the youth. Stories of military exploits were repeated almost before boys left their mother's breast. Does a little booby cry for any ache? The mother scolds him in this fashion: 'What a coward to cry for a trifling pain! What will you do when your arm is cut off in battle? What when you are called upon to commit *hara kiri*?' We all know the pathetic fortitude of a famished little boy-prince of Sendai, who in the drama is made to say to his little page, 'Seest thou those tiny sparrows in the nest, how their yellow bills are opened wide, and now see! there comes their mother with worms to feed them. How eagerly and happily the little ones eat! but for a samurai, when his stomach is empty, it is a disgrace to feel hunger.' Anecdotes of fortitude and bravery abound in nursery tales, though stories of this kind are not by any means the only method of early imbuing the spirit with daring and fearlessness. Parents, with sternness sometimes verging on cruelty, set their children to tasks that called forth all the pluck that was in them. 'Bears hurl their cubs down the gorge,' they said. Samurai's sons were let down the steep valleys of hardship, and spurred to Sisyphus-like tasks. Occasional deprivation of food or exposure to cold, was considered a highly efficacious test for inuring them to endurance. Children of tender age were sent among utter strangers with some message to deliver, were made to rise before the sun, and before breakfast attend to their reading exercises, walking to their teacher with bare feet in the cold of winter; they frequently – once or twice a month, as on the festival of a god of learning – came together in small groups and passed the night without sleep, in reading aloud by turns. Pilgrimages to all sorts of uncanny places – to execution grounds, to graveyards, to houses reputed to be haunted, were favourite pastimes of the young. In the days when decapitation was public, not only were small boys sent to witness the ghastly scene, but they were made to visit alone the place in the darkness of night and there to leave a mark of their visit on the trunkless head.

Does this ultra-Spartan system of 'drilling the nerves' strike the modern pedagogist with horror and doubt – doubt whether the tendency would not be brutalizing, nipping in the bud the tender emotions of the heart? Let us see what other concepts Bushido had of Valour.

The spiritual aspect of valour is evidenced by composure – calm presence of mind. Tranquillity is courage in repose. It is a statical manifestation of valour, as daring deeds are a dynamical. A truly brave man is ever serene; he is never taken by surprise; nothing ruffles the equanimity of his spirit. In the heat of battle he remains cool; in the midst of catastrophes he keeps level his mind. Earthquakes do not shake him, he laughs at storms. We admire him as truly great, who, in the menacing presence of danger or death, retains his self-possession; who, for instance, can compose a poem under impending peril or hum a strain in the face of death. Such indulgence betraying no tremor in the writing or in the voice, is taken as an infallible index of a large nature – of what we call a capacious mind (*yoyu*), which, far from being pressed or crowded, has always room for something more.

There is even a sportive element in a courageous nature. Things which are serious to ordinary people, may be but play to the valiant. Hence in old warfare it was not at all rare for the parties to a conflict to exchange repartee or to begin a rhetorical contest. Combat was not solely a matter of brute force; it was, as well, an intellectual engagement.

The sorrow which overtook Antony and Octavius at the death of Brutus, has been the general experience of brave men. Kenshin, who fought for fourteen years with Shingen, when he heard of the latter's death, wept aloud at the loss of 'the best of enemies.' Nietzsche spoke for the samurai heart when he wrote, 'You are to be proud of your enemy; then, the success of your enemy is your success also.' Indeed valour and honour alike required that we should own as enemies in war only such as prove worthy of being friends in peace. When valour attains this height, it becomes akin to Benevolence.

CHAPTER FIVE

Benevolence, the Feeling of Distress

Love, magnanimity, affection for others, sympathy and pity, were ever recognized to be supreme virtues, the highest of all the attributes of the human soul. It was deemed a princely virtue in a twofold sense: princely among the manifold attributes of a noble spirit; princely as particularly befitting a princely profession. We needed no Shakespeare to feel – though, perhaps, like the rest of the world, we needed him to express it – that mercy became a monarch better than his crown, that it was above his sceptred sway. How often both Confucius and Mencius repeat the highest requirement of a ruler of men to consist in benevolence. Confucius would say, 'Let but a prince cultivate virtue, people will flock to him; with people will come to him lands; lands will bring forth for him wealth; wealth will give him the benefit of right uses. Virtue is the root, and wealth an outcome.' Again, 'Never has there been a case of a sovereign loving benevolence, and the people not loving righteousness.' Mencius follows close at his heels and says, 'Instances are on record where individuals attained to supreme power in a single state, without benevolence, but never have I heard of a whole empire falling into the hands of one who lacked this virtue. Also, it is impossible that any one should become ruler of the people to whom they have not yielded the subjection of their hearts.' Both defined this indispensable requirement in a ruler by saying, 'Benevolence – benevolence is Man.'

Under the regime of feudalism, which could easily degenerate into militarism, it was to benevolence that we owed our deliverance from despotism of the worst kind. An utter surrender of 'life and limb' on the part of the governed would have left nothing for the governing but self-will, and this has for its natural consequence the growth of that absolutism so often called 'oriental despotism,' as though there were no despots of occidental history!

Let it be far from me to uphold despotism of any sort; but it is a mistake to identify feudalism with it. When Frederick the Great wrote that 'Kings are the first servants of the State,' jurists thought rightly that a new era was reached in the development of freedom. Strangely coinciding in time, in the backwoods of North-western Japan, Yozan of Yonézawa made exactly the same declaration, showing that feudalism was not all tyranny and oppression. A feudal prince, although unmindful of owing reciprocal obligations to his vassals, felt a higher sense of responsibility to his ancestors and to Heaven. He was a father to his subjects, whom Heaven entrusted to his care. According to the ancient Chinese *Book of Poetry*, 'Until the house of Yin lost the hearts of the people, they could appear before Heaven.' And Confucius in his *Great Learning* taught: 'When the prince loves what the people love and hates what the people hate, then is he what is called the parent of the people.' Thus are public opinion and monarchical will or democracy and absolutism merged one in the other. Thus also, in a sense not usually assigned to the term, Bushido accepted and corroborated paternal government – paternal also as opposed to the less interested avuncular government. (Uncle Sam's, to wit!) The difference between a despotic and a paternal government lies in this, that in the one the people obey reluctantly, while in the other they do so with 'that proud submission, that dignified obedience, that subordination of heart which kept alive, even in servitude itself, the spirit of exalted freedom.'[7]

Virtue and absolute power may strike the Anglo-Saxon mind as terms which it is impossible to harmonise. Pobyedonostseff has clearly set forth before us the contrast in the foundations of English and other European communities; namely,

that these were organized on the basis of common interest, while that was distinguished by a strongly developed independent personality. What this Russian statesman says of the personal dependence of individuals on some social alliance and in the end of ends on the State, among the continental nations of Europe and particularly among Slavonic peoples, is doubly true of the Japanese. Hence not only is a free exercise of monarchical power not felt as heavily by us as in Europe, but it is generally moderated by paternal consideration for the feelings of the people. 'Absolutism,' says Bismarck, 'primarily demands in the ruler impartiality, honesty, devotion to duty, energy and inward humility.' If I may be allowed to make one more quotation on this subject, I will cite from the speech of the German Emperor at Koblenz, in which he spoke of 'Kingship, by the grace of God, with its heavy duties, its tremendous responsibilities to the Creator alone, from which no man, no minister, no parliament, can release the monarch.'

We knew benevolence was a tender virtue and mother-like. If upright Rectitude and stem justice were peculiarly masculine, Mercy had the gentleness and the persuasiveness of a feminine nature. We were warned against indulging in indiscriminate charity, without seasoning it with justice and rectitude. Masamuné expressed it well in his oft-quoted aphorism – 'Rectitude carried to excess hardens into stiffness; benevolence indulged beyond measure sinks into weakness.' Fortunately mercy was not so rare as it was beautiful, for it is universally true that 'The bravest are the tenderest, the loving are the daring.' '*Bushi no nasaké*' – the tenderness of a warrior – had a sound which appealed at once to whatever was noble in us; not that the mercy of a samurai was generically different from the mercy of any other being, but because it implied mercy where mercy was not a blind impulse, but where it recognized due regard to justice, and where mercy did not remain merely a certain state of mind, but where it was backed with power to save or kill. As economists speak of demand as being effectual or ineffectual, similarly we may call the mercy of Bushi effectual, since it implied the power of acting for the good or detriment of the recipient.

Priding themselves as they did in their brute strength and privileges to turn it into account, the samurai gave full consent to what Mencius taught concerning the power of love. 'Benevolence,' he says, 'brings under its sway whatever hinders its power, just as water subdues fire: they only doubt the power of water to quench flames who try to extinguish with a cupful a whole burning waggon-load of faggots.' He also says that 'the feeling of distress is the root of benevolence,' therefore a benevolent man is ever mindful of those who are suffering and in distress. Thus did Mencius long anticipate Adam Smith, who founds his ethical philosophy on sympathy.

It is indeed striking how closely the code of knightly honour of one country coincides with that of others; in other words, how the much-abused oriental ideas of morals find their counterparts in the noblest maxims of European literature. If the well-known lines,

Hae tibi erunt artes – pacisque imponere morem,
Parcere subjectis, et debellare superbos,[8]

were shown to a Japanese gentleman, he might readily accuse the Mantuan bard of plagiarizing from the literature of his own country.

Benevolence to the weak, the down-trodden or the vanquished, was ever extolled as peculiarly becoming to a samurai. Lovers of Japanese art must be familiar with the representation of a priest riding backwards on a cow. The rider was once a warrior who in his day made his name a by-word of terror. In that terrible battle of Sumano-ura (AD1184), which was one of the most decisive in our history, he overtook an enemy and in single combat had him in the clutch of his gigantic arms. Now the etiquette of war required that on such occasions no blood should be spilt, unless the weaker party proved to be a man of rank or ability equal to that of the stronger. The grim combatant would have the name of the man under him; but he refusing to make it known, his helmet was ruthlessly torn off, when the sight of a juvenile face, fair and beardless, made the astonished knight relax his hold. Helping the youth to his feet, in paternal tones he bade the stripling go: 'Off, young prince, to thy mother's side! The sword of Kumagayé shall never be tarnished by a drop of thy blood. Haste and flee o'er yon pass before thine enemies come in sight!' The young warrior refused to go and begged Kumagayé, for the honour of both, to dispatch him on the spot. Above the hoary head of the veteran gleams the cold blade, which many a time before has sundered the chords of life, but his stout heart quails; there flashes athwart his mental eye the vision of his own boy, who this self-same day marched to the sound of bugle to try his maiden arms; the strong hand of the warrior quivers; again he begs his victim to flee for his life. Finding all his entreaties vain and hearing the approaching steps of his comrades, he exclaims: 'If thou art overtaken, thou mayst fall at a more ignoble hand than mine. O thou Infinite! receive his soul!' In an instant the sword flashes in the air, and when it falls it is red with adolescent blood. When the war is ended, we find our soldier returning in triumph, but little cares he now for honour or fame; he renounces his warlike career, shaves his head, dons a priestly garb, devotes the rest of his days to holy pilgrimage, never turning his back to the West where lies the Paradise whence salvation comes and whither the sun hastes daily for his rest.

Critics may point out flaws in this story, which is casuistically vulnerable. Let it be: all the same it shows that Tenderness, Pity, and Love were traits which adorned the most sanguinary exploits of a samurai. It was an old maxim among them that 'It becometh not the fowler to slay the bird which takes refuge in his bosom.' This in a large measure explains why the Red Cross movement, considered so peculiarly Christian, so readily found a firm footing among us. Decades before we heard of the Geneva Convention, Bakin, our greatest novelist, had familiarized us with the medical treatment of a fallen foe. In the principality of Satsuma, noted for its martial spirit and education, the custom prevailed for young men to practise music; not the blast of trumpets or the beat of drums – 'those clamorous harbingers of blood and death' – stirring us to imitate the actions of a tiger, but sad and tender melodies on the *biwa*,[9] soothing our fiery spirits, drawing our thoughts away from scent of blood and scenes of carnage.

Nor was Satsuma the only place in Japan where gentleness was inculcated among the warrior class. A Prince of Shirakawa jots down his random thoughts, and among them is the following: 'Though they come stealing to your bedside in the silent watches of the night, drive not away, but rather cherish these – the fragrance of flowers, the sound of distant bells, the insect hummings of a frosty night.' And again, 'Though they may wound your feelings, these three you have only to forgive, the breeze that scatters your flowers, the cloud that hides your moon, and the man who tries to pick quarrels with you.'

It was ostensibly to express, but actually to cultivate, these gentler emotions that the writing of verses was encouraged. Our poetry has therefore a strong undercurrent of pathos and tenderness. A well-known anecdote of a rustic samurai illustrates the case in point. When he was told to learn versification, and 'The Warbler's Notes'[10] was given him for the subject of his first attempt, his fiery spirit rebelled and he flung at the feet of his master this uncouth production, which ran:

> *'The brave warrior keeps apart*
> *The ear that might listen*
> *To the warbler's song.'*

His master, undaunted by the crude sentiment, continued to encourage the youth, until one day the music of his soul was awakened to respond to the sweet notes of the *uguisu*, and he wrote:

> *'Stands the warrior, mailed and strong,*
> *To hear the uguisu's song,*
> *Warbled sweet the trees among.'*

We admire and enjoy the heroic incident in Korner's short life, when, as he lay wounded on the battlefield, he scribbled his famous *Farewell to Life*. Incidents of a similar kind were not at all unusual in our warfare. Our pithy, epigrammatic poems were particularly well suited to the improvization of a single sentiment. Everybody of any education was either a poet or a poetaster. Not infrequently a marching soldier might be seen to halt, take his writing utensils from his belt, and compose an ode – and such papers were found afterward in the helmets or the breastplates when these were removed from their lifeless wearers.

What Christianity has done in Europe toward rousing compassion in the midst of belligerent horrors, love of music and letters has done in Japan. The cultivation of tender feelings breeds considerate regard for the sufferings of others. Modesty and complaisance, actuated by respect for others' feelings, are at the root of politeness.

CHAPTER SIX

Politeness

Courtesy and urbanity of manners have been noticed by every foreign tourist as a marked Japanese trait. Politeness is a poor virtue, if it is actuated only by a fear of offending good taste, whereas it should be the outward manifestation of a sympathetic regard for the feelings of others. It also implies a due regard for the fitness of things, therefore due respect to social positions; for these latter express no plutocratic distinctions, but were originally distinctions for actual merit.

In its highest form, politeness almost approaches love. We may reverently say, politeness 'suffereth long, and is kind; envieth not, vaunteth not itself, is not puffed up; doth not behave itself unseemly, seeketh not her own, is not easily provoked, taketh not account of evil.' Is it any wonder that Professor Dean, in speaking of the six elements of Humanity, accords to politeness an exalted position, inasmuch as it is the ripest fruit of social intercourse?

While thus extolling politeness, far be it from me to put it in the front rank of virtues. If we analyze it, we shall find it correlated with other virtues of a higher order; for what virtue stands alone? While – or rather because – it was exalted as peculiar to the profession of arms, and as such esteemed in a degree higher than its deserts, there came into existence its counterfeits. Confucius himself has repeatedly taught that external appurtenances are as little a part of propriety as sounds are of music.

When propriety was elevated to the *sine qua non* of social intercourse, it was only to be expected that an elaborate system of etiquette should come into vogue to train youth in correct social behaviour. How one must bow in accosting others, how he must walk and sit, were taught and learned with utmost care. Table manners grew to be a science. Tea serving and drinking were raised to a ceremony. A man of education is, of course, expected to be master of all these.

I have heard slighting remarks made by Europeans upon our elaborate discipline of politeness. It has been criticized as absorbing too much of our thought and in so far a folly to observe strict obedience to it. I admit that there may be unnecessary niceties in ceremonious etiquette, but whether it partakes as much of folly as the adherence to ever-changing fashions of the West, is a question not very clear to my mind. Even fashions I do not consider solely as freaks of vanity; on the contrary, I look upon these as a ceaseless search of the human mind for the beautiful. Much less do I consider elaborate ceremony as altogether trivial; for it denotes the result of long observation as to the most appropriate method of achieving a certain result. If there is anything to do, there is certainly a best way to do it, and the best way is both the most economical and the most graceful. Mr. Spencer defines grace as the most economical manner of motion. The tea ceremony presents certain definite ways of manipulating a bowl, a spoon, a napkin, etc. To a novice it looks tedious. But one soon discovers that the way prescribed is, after all, the most saving of time and labour; in other words, the most economical use of force – hence, according to Spencer's dictum, the most graceful.

I have said that etiquette was elaborated into the finest niceties, so much so that different schools advocating different systems, came into existence. But they all united in the ultimate essential, and this was put by a great exponent of the best known school of etiquette, the Ogasawara, in the following terms: 'The end of all etiquette is to so cultivate your mind that even when you are quietly seated, not the roughest ruffian can dare make onset on your person.' It means, in other words, that by constant exercise in correct manners, one brings all the parts and faculties of his body into perfect order and into such harmony with itself and its environment as to express the mastery of spirit over the flesh. What a new and deep significance the French word *bienséance*[11] comes thus to contain!

If the premise is true that gracefulness means economy of force, then it follows as a logical sequence that a constant practice of graceful deportment must bring with it a reserve and storage of force. Fine manners, therefore, mean power in repose.

As an example of how the simplest thing can be made into an art and then become spiritual culture, I may take *Cha-no-yu*, the tea ceremony. Tea-sipping as a fine art! Why should it not be? In the children drawing pictures on the sand, or in the savage carving on a rock, was the promise of a Raphael or a Michelangelo. How much more is the drinking of a beverage, which began with the transcendental contemplation of a Hindu anchorite, entitled to develop into a handmaid of Religion and Morality? That calmness of mind, that serenity of temper, that composure and quietness of demeanour, which are the first essentials of *Cha-no-yu*, are without doubt the first conditions of right thinking and right feeling. The scrupulous cleanliness of the little room, shut off from sight and sound of the madding crowd, is in itself conducive to direct one's thoughts from the world. The bare interior does not engross one's attention like the innumerable pictures and bric-a-brac of a Western parlour; the presence of *kakémono*[12] calls our attention more to grace of design than to beauty of colour. The utmost refinement of taste is the object aimed at; whereas anything like display is banished with religious horror. The very fact that it was invented by a contemplative recluse, in a time when wars and the rumours of wars were incessant, is well calculated to show that this institution was more than a pastime. Before entering the quiet precincts of the tea-room, the company assembling to partake of the ceremony laid aside, together with their swords, the ferocity of the battlefield or the cares of government, there to find peace and friendship.

Cha-no-yu is more than a ceremony – it is a fine art; it is poetry, with articulate gestures for rhythm: it is a *modus operandi* of soul discipline. Its greatest value lies in this last phase. Not infrequently the other phases preponderated in the mind of its votaries, but that does not prove that its essence was not of a spiritual nature.

Politeness will be a great acquisition, if it does no more than impart grace to manners; but its function does not stop here. For propriety, springing as it does from motives of benevolence and modesty, and actuated by tender feelings toward the sensibilities of others, is ever a graceful expression of sympathy. Its requirement is that we should weep with those that weep and rejoice with those that rejoice. Such didactic requirement, when reduced into small everyday details of life, expresses itself in little acts scarcely noticeable, or, if noticed, is, as one missionary lady of twenty years' residence once said to me, 'awfully funny.' You are out in the hot glaring sun with no shade over you; a Japanese acquaintance passes by; you accost him, and instantly his hat is off – well, that is perfectly natural, but the 'awfully funny' performance is, that all the while he talks with you his parasol is down and he stands in the glaring sun also. How foolish! – Yes, exactly so, provided the motive were less than this: 'You are in the sun; I sympathize with you; I would willingly take you under my parasol if it were large enough, or if we were familiarly acquainted; as I cannot shade you, I will share your discomforts.' Little acts of this kind, equally or more amusing, are not mere gestures or conventionalities. They are the 'bodying forth' of thoughtful feelings for the comfort of others.

Another 'awfully funny' custom is dictated by our canons of politeness; but many superficial writers on Japan have dismissed it by simply attributing it to the general topsy-turvyness of the nation. Every foreigner who has observed it will confess the awkwardness he felt in making proper reply upon the occasion. In America, when you make a gift, you sing its praises to the recipient; in Japan we depreciate or slander it. The underlying idea with you is, 'This is a nice gift: if it were not nice I would not dare give it to you; for it will be an insult to give you anything but what is nice.' In contrast to this, our logic runs: 'You are a nice person, and no gift is nice enough for you. You will not accept anything I can lay at your feet except as a token of my good will; so accept this, not for its intrinsic value, but as a token. It will be an insult to your worth to call the best gift good enough for you.' Place the two ideas side by side; and we see that the ultimate idea is one and the same. Neither is 'awfully funny.' The American speaks of the material which makes the gift; the Japanese speaks of the spirit which prompts the gift.

It is perverse reasoning to conclude, because our sense of propriety shows itself in all the smallest ramifications of our deportment, to take the least important

of them and uphold it as the type, and pass judgment upon the principle itself. Which is more important, to eat or to observe rules of propriety about eating? A Chinese sage answers, 'If you take a case where the eating is all-important, and observing the rules of propriety is of little importance, and compare them together, why merely say that the eating is of the more importance?' 'Metal is heavier than feathers,' but does that saying have reference to a single clasp of metal and a wagon-load of feathers? Take a piece of wood a foot thick and raise it above the pinnacle of a temple, none would call it taller than the temple. To the question, 'Which is the more important, to tell the truth or to be polite?' the Japanese are said to give an answer diametrically opposite to what the American will say – but I forbear any comment until I come to speak of veracity and sincerity.

CHAPTER SEVEN

Veracity and Sincerity

Without veracity and sincerity, politeness is a farce and a show. 'Propriety carried beyond right bounds,' says Masamuné, 'becomes a lie.' An ancient poet has outdone Polonius in the advice he gives: 'To thyself be faithful: if in thy heart thou strayest not from truth, without prayer of thine the Gods will keep thee whole.' The apotheosis of Sincerity to which Confucius gives expression in the *Doctrine of the Mean*, attributes to it transcendental powers, almost identifying them with the Divine. 'Sincerity is the end and the beginning of all things; without Sincerity there would be nothing.' He then dwells with eloquence on its far-reaching and long-enduring nature, its power to produce changes without movement and by its mere presence to accomplish its purpose without effort. From the Chinese ideogram for Sincerity, which is a combination of 'Word' and 'Perfect,' one is tempted to draw a parallel between it and the Neo-Platonic doctrine of *Logos* – to such height does the sage soar in his unwonted mystic flight.

Lying or equivocation were deemed equally cowardly. The bushi held that his high social position demanded a loftier standard of veracity than that of the tradesman and peasant. *Bushi no ichi-gon* – the word of a samurai, or in exact German equivalent *ein Ritterwort* – was sufficient guaranty of the truthfulness of an assertion. His word carried such weight with it that promises were generally made and fulfilled without a written pledge, which would have been deemed quite beneath his dignity. Many thrilling anecdotes were told of those who atoned by death for *ni-gon*, a double tongue.

The regard for veracity was so high that, unlike the generality of Christians who persistently violate the plain commands of the Teacher not to swear, the best of samurai looked upon an oath as derogatory to their honour. I am well aware that they did swear by different deities or upon their swords; but never has swearing degenerated into wanton form and irreverent interjection. To emphasize our words a practice was sometimes resorted to of literally sealing with blood. For the explanation of such a practice, I need only refer my readers to Goethe's *Faust*.

A recent American writer is responsible for this statement, that if you ask an ordinary Japanese which is better, to tell a falsehood or be impolite, he will not hesitate to answer 'to tell a falsehood!' Dr. Peery[13] is partly right and partly wrong; right in that an ordinary Japanese, even a samurai, may answer in the way ascribed to him, but wrong in attributing too much weight to the term he translates 'falsehood.' This word (in Japanese, *uso*) is employed to denote anything which is not a truth (*makoto*) or fact (*honto*). Lowell tells us that Wordsworth could not distinguish between truth and fact, and an ordinary Japanese is in this respect as good as Wordsworth. Ask a Japanese, or even an American of any refinement, to tell you whether he dislikes you or whether he is sick at his stomach, and he will not hesitate long to tell falsehoods and answer, 'I like you much,' or, 'I am quite well, thank you.' To sacrifice truth merely for the sake of politeness was regarded as an 'empty form' (*kyo-rei*) and 'deception by sweet words.'

I own I am speaking now of the Bushido idea of veracity; but it may not be amiss to devote a few words to our commercial integrity, of which I have heard much complaint in foreign books and journals. A loose business morality has indeed been the worst blot on our national reputation; but before abusing it or hastily condemning the whole race for it, let us calmly study it and we shall be rewarded with consolation for the future.

Of all the great occupations of life, none was farther removed from the profession of arms than commerce. The merchant was placed lowest in the category of vocations – the knight, the tiller of the soil, the mechanic, the merchant. The samurai derived his income from land and could even indulge, if he had a mind to, in amateur farming; but the counter and abacus were abhorred. We know the wisdom of this social arrangement. Montesquieu has made it clear that the debarring of the nobility from mercantile pursuits was an admirable social policy, in that it prevented wealth from accumulating in the hands of the powerful. The separation of power and riches kept the distribution of the latter more nearly equable. Professor Dill, the author of *Roman Society in the Last Century of the Western Empire*, has brought afresh to our mind that one cause of the decadence of the Roman Empire, was the permission given to the nobility to engage in trade, and the consequent monopoly of wealth and power by a minority of the senatorial families.

Commerce, therefore, in feudal Japan did not reach that degree of development which it would have attained under freer conditions. The obloquy attached to the calling naturally brought within its pale such as cared little for social repute. 'Call one a thief and he will steal.' Put a stigma on a calling and its followers adjust their morals to it, for it is natural that 'the normal conscience,' as Hugh Black says, 'rises to the demands made on it, and easily falls to the limit of the standard expected from it.' It is unnecessary to add that no business, commercial or otherwise, can be transacted without a code of morals. Our merchants of the feudal period had one among themselves, without which they could never have developed, as they did in embryo, such fundamental mercantile institutions as the guild, the bank, the bourse, insurance, checks, bills of exchange, etc.; but in their relations with people outside their vocation, the tradesmen lived too true to the reputation of their order.

This being the case, when the country was opened to foreign trade, only the most adventurous and unscrupulous rushed to the ports, while the respectable business houses declined for some time the repeated requests of the authorities to establish branch houses. Was Bushido powerless to stay the current of commercial dishonour? Let us see.

Those who are well acquainted with our history will remember that only a few years after our treaty ports were opened to foreign trade, feudalism was abolished, and when with it the samurai's fiefs were taken and bonds issued to them in compensation, they were given liberty to invest them in mercantile

transactions. Now you may ask, 'Why could they not bring their much-boasted veracity into their new business relations and so reform the old abuses?' Those who had eyes to see could not weep enough, those who had hearts to feel could not sympathize enough, with the fate of many a noble and honest samurai who signally and irrevocably failed in his new and unfamiliar field of trade and industry, through sheer lack of shrewdness in coping with his artful plebeian rival. When we know that eighty per cent of the business houses fail in so industrial a country as America, is it any wonder that scarcely one among a hundred samurai who went into trade could succeed in his new vocation? It will be long before it will be recognized how many fortunes were wrecked in the attempt to apply Bushido ethics to business methods; but it was soon patent to every observing mind that the ways of wealth were not the ways of honour. In what respects, then, were they different?

Of the three incentives to veracity that Lecky enumerates, viz., the industrial, the political, and the philosophical, the first was altogether lacking in Bushido. As to the second, it could develop little in a political community under a feudal system. It is in its philosophical and, as Lecky says, in its highest aspect, that honesty attained elevated rank in our catalogue of virtues. With all my sincere regard for the high commercial integrity of the Anglo-Saxon race, when I ask for the ultimate ground, I am told that 'honesty is the best policy' – that it *pays* to be honest. Is not this virtue, then, its own reward? If it is followed because it brings in more cash than falsehood, I am afraid Bushido would rather indulge in lies!

If Bushido rejects a doctrine of *quid pro quo* rewards, the shrewder tradesman will readily accept it. Lecky has very truly remarked that veracity owes its growth largely to commerce and manufacture; as Nietzsche puts it, honesty is the youngest of the virtues – in other words, it is the foster-child of modern industry. Without this mother, veracity was like a blue-blood orphan whom only the most cultivated mind could adopt and nourish. Such minds were general among the samurai, but, for want of a more democratic and utilitarian foster-mother, the tender child failed to thrive. Industries advancing, veracity will prove an easy, nay, a profitable virtue to practise. Just think – as late as November, 1880, Bismarck sent a circular to the professional consuls of the

German Empire, warning them of 'a lamentable lack of reliability with regard to German shipments *inter alia*, apparent both as to quality and quantity.' Nowadays we hear comparatively little of German carelessness and dishonesty in trade. In twenty years her merchants have learned that in the end honesty pays. Already our merchants have found that out.

Often have I wondered whether the veracity of Bushido had any motive higher than courage. In the absence of any positive commandment against bearing false witness, lying was not condemned as sin, but simply denounced as weakness, and, as such, highly dishonourable. As a matter of fact, the idea of honesty is so intimately blended, and its Latin and its German etymology so identified with honour, that it is high time I should pause a few moments for the consideration of this feature of the Precepts of Knighthood.

CHAPTER EIGHT

Honour

The sense of honour, implying a vivid consciousness of personal dignity and worth, could not fail to characterize the samurai, born and bred to value the duties and privileges of their profession. Though the word ordinarily given nowadays as the translation of honour was not used freely, yet the idea was conveyed by such terms as *na* (name) *men-moku* (countenance), *guai-bun* (outside hearing), reminding us respectively of the biblical use of 'name,' of the evolution of the term 'personality' from the Greek mask, and of 'fame.' A good name – one's reputation, 'the immortal part of one's self, what remains being bestial' – assumed as a matter of course, any infringement upon its integrity was felt as shame, and the sense of shame (*Ren-chi-shin*) was one of the earliest to be cherished in juvenile education. 'You will be laughed at,' 'It will disgrace you,' 'Are you not ashamed?' were the last appeal to correct behaviour on the part of a youthful delinquent. Such a recourse to his honour touched the most sensitive spot in the child's heart, as though it had been nursed on honour while he was in his mother's womb; for most truly is honour a pre-natal influence, being closely bound up with strong family consciousness. 'In losing the solidarity of families,' says Balzac, 'society has lost the fundamental force which Montesquieu named Honour.' Indeed, the sense of shame seems to me to be the earliest indication of the moral consciousness of the race. The first and worst punishment which befell humanity in consequence of tasting 'the fruit of that forbidden tree' was,

to my mind, not the sorrow of childbirth, nor the thorns and thistles, but the awakening of the sense of shame. Few incidents in history excel in pathos the scene of the first mother plying, with heaving breast and tremulous fingers, her crude needle on the few fig leaves which her dejected husband plucked for her. This first fruit of disobedience clings to us with a tenacity that nothing else does. All the sartorial ingenuity of mankind has not yet succeeded in sewing an apron that will efficaciously hide our sense of shame. That samurai was right who refused to compromise his character by a slight humiliation in his youth; 'because,' he said, 'dishonour is like a scar on a tree, which time, instead of effacing, only helps to enlarge.'

Mencius had taught centuries before, in almost the identical phrase, what Carlyle has latterly expressed – namely, that 'Shame is the soil of all Virtue, of good manners and good morals.'

The fear of disgrace was so great that if our literature lacks such eloquence as Shakespeare puts into the mouth of Norfolk, it nevertheless hung like Damocles' sword over the head of every samurai and often assumed a morbid character. In the name of honour, deeds were perpetrated which can find no justification in the code of Bushido. At the slightest, nay – imaginary insult – the quick-tempered braggart took offence, resorted to the use of the sword, and many an unnecessary strife was raised and many an innocent life lost. The story of a well-meaning citizen who called the attention of a bushi to a flea jumping on his back, and who was forthwith cut in two, for the simple and questionable reason, that inasmuch as fleas are parasites which feed on animals, it was an unpardonable insult to identify a noble warrior with a beast – I say, stories like these are too frivolous to believe. Yet, the circulation of such stories implies three things: (1) that they were invented to overawe common people; (2) that abuses were really made of the samurai's profession of honour; and (3) that a very strong sense of shame was developed among them. It is plainly unfair to take an abnormal case to cast blame upon the precepts, any more than to judge of the true teachings of Christ from the fruits of religious fanaticism and extravagance – inquisitions and hypocrisy. But, as in religious monomania there is something touchingly noble as compared with the delirium tremens of a drunkard, so in that extreme sensitiveness of the samurai about their honour do we not recognize the substratum of a genuine virtue?

The morbid excess into which the delicate code of honour was inclined to run was strongly counterbalanced by preaching magnanimity and patience. To take offence at slight provocation was ridiculed as 'short-tempered.' The popular adage said: 'To bear what you think you cannot bear is really to bear.' The great Iyéyasu left to posterity a few maxims, among which are the following: 'The life of man is like going a long distance with a heavy load upon the shoulders. Haste not... Reproach none, but be forever watchful of thine own short-comings... Forbearance is the basis of length of days.' He proved in his life what he preached. A literary wit put a characteristic epigram into the mouths of three well-known personages in our history: to Nobunaga he attributed, 'I will kill her, if the nightingale sings not in time'; to Hidéyoshi, 'I will force her to sing for me'; and to Iyéyasu, 'I will wait till she opens her lips.'

Patience and long-suffering were also highly commended by Mencius. In one place he writes to this effect: 'Though you denude yourself and insult me, what is that to me? You cannot defile my soul by your outrage.' Elsewhere he teaches that anger at a petty offence is unworthy of a superior man, but indignation for a great cause is righteous wrath.

To what height of unmartial and unresisting meekness Bushido could reach in some of its votaries, may be seen in their utterances. Take, for instance, this saying of Ogawa: 'When others speak all manner of evil things against thee, return not evil for evil, but rather reflect that thou wast not more faithful in the discharge of thy duties.' Take another of Kumazawa: 'When others blame thee, blame them not; when others are angry at thee, return not anger. Joy cometh only as Passion and Desire part.' Still another instance I may cite from Saigo, upon whose overhanging brows 'Shame is ashamed to sit': 'The Way is the way of Heaven and Earth; Man's place is to follow it; therefore make it the object of thy life to reverence Heaven. Heaven loves me and others with equal love; therefore with the love wherewith thou lovest thyself, love others. Make not Man thy partner but Heaven, and making Heaven thy partner do thy best. Never condemn others; but see to it that thou comest not short of thine own mark.' Some of these sayings remind us of Christian expostulations, and show us how far in practical morality natural religion can approach the revealed. Not only did these sayings remain as utterances, but they were really embodied in acts.

It must be admitted that very few attained this sublime height of magnanimity, patience and forgiveness. It was a great pity that nothing clear and general was expressed as to what constitutes honour, only a few enlightened minds being aware that it 'from no condition rises,' but that it lies in each acting well his part; for nothing was easier than for youths to forget in the heat of action what they had learned in Mencius in their calmer moments. Said this sage: ''Tis in every man's mind to love honour; but little doth he dream that what is truly honourable lies within himself and not elsewhere. The honour which men confer is not good honour. Those whom Châo the Great ennobles, he can make mean again.' For the most part, an insult was quickly resented and repaid by death, as we shall see later, while honour – too often nothing higher than vainglory or worldly approbation – was prized as the *summum bonum* of earthly existence. Fame, and not wealth or knowledge, was the goal toward which youths had to strive. Many a lad swore within himself as he crossed the threshold of his paternal home, that he would not recross it until he had made a name in the world; and many an ambitious mother refused to see her sons again unless they could 'return home,' as the expression is, 'caparisoned in brocade.' To shun shame or win a name, samurai boys would submit to any privations and undergo the severest ordeals of bodily or mental suffering. They knew that honour won

in youth grows with age. In the memorable seige of Osaka, a young son of Iyéyasu, in spite of his earnest entreaties to be put in the vanguard, was placed at the rear of the army. When the castle fell, he was so chagrined and wept so bitterly that an old councillor tried to console him with all the resources at his command; 'Take comfort, Sire,' said he, 'at the thought of the long future before you. In the many years that you may live, there will come divers occasions to distinguish yourself.' The boy fixed his indignant gaze upon the man and said, 'How foolishly you talk! Can ever my fourteenth year come round again?' Life itself was thought cheap if honour and fame could be attained therewith: hence, whenever a cause presented itself which was considered dearer than life, with utmost serenity and celerity was life laid down.

Of the causes in comparison with which no life was too dear to sacrifice, was the duty of loyalty, which was the key-stone making feudal virtues a symmetrical arch.

CHAPTER NINE

The Duty of Loyalty

Feudal morality shares other virtues in common with other systems of ethics, with other classes of people, but this virtue – homage and fealty to a superior – is its distinctive feature. I am aware that personal fidelity is a moral adhesion existing among all sorts and conditions of men – a gang of pickpockets owe allegiance to a Fagin; but it is only in the code of chivalrous honour that loyalty assumes paramount importance.

In spite of Hegel's criticism[14] that the fidelity of feudal vassals, being an obligation to an individual and not to a commonwealth, is a bond established on totally unjust principles, a great compatriot of his made it his boast that personal loyalty was a German virtue. Bismarck had good reasons to do so, not because the *Treue* he boasts of was the monopoly of his Fatherland or of any single nation or race, but because this favoured fruit of chivalry lingers latest among the people where feudalism has lasted longest. In America, where 'everybody is as good as anybody else,' and, as the Irishman added, 'better too,' such exalted ideas of loyalty as we feel for our sovereign may be deemed 'excellent within certain bounds,' but preposterous as encouraged among us. Montesquieu complained long ago that right on one side of the Pyrenees was wrong on the other, and the recent Dreyfus trial[15] proved the truth of his remark, save that the Pyrenees were not the sole boundary beyond which French justice finds no accord. Similarly, loyalty as we conceive it may find few admirers elsewhere, not because our conception is wrong, but because it is, I am afraid, forgotten, and also because we carry it to a degree not reached in any other country. Griffis[16] was quite right in stating that whereas in China Confucian ethics made obedience to parents the primary human duty, in Japan precedence was given to loyalty. At the risk of shocking some of my good readers, I will relate of one 'who could endure to follow a fall'n lord' and who thus, as Shakespeare assures, 'earned a place i' the story.'

The story is of one of the greatest characters of our history, Michizané, who, falling a victim to jealousy and calumny, is exiled from the capital. Not content with this, his unrelenting enemies are now bent upon the extinction of his family. Strict search for his son – not yet grown – reveals the fact of his being secreted in a village school kept by one Genzo, a former vassal of Michizané. When orders are dispatched to the schoolmaster to deliver the head of the juvenile offender on a certain day, his first idea is to find a suitable substitute for it. He ponders over his school-list, scrutinizes with careful eyes all the boys, as they stroll into the class-room, but none among the children born of the soil bears the least resemblance to his protégé. His despair, however, is but for a moment; for, behold, a new scholar is announced – a comely boy of the same age as his master's son, escorted by a mother of noble mien.

No less conscious of the resemblance between infant lord and infant retainer, were the mother and the boy himself. In the privacy of home both had laid themselves upon the altar; the one his life – the other her heart, yet without sign to the outer world. Unwitting of what had passed between them, it is the teacher from whom comes the suggestion.

Here, then, is the scapegoat! The rest of the narrative may be briefly told. On the day appointed, arrives the officer commissioned to identify and receive the head of the youth. Will he be deceived by the false head? The poor Genzo's hand is on the hilt of the sword, ready to strike a blow either at the man or at himself, should the examination defeat his scheme. The officer takes up the gruesome object before him, goes calmly over each feature, and in a deliberate, business-like tone, pronounces it genuine. That evening in a lonely home awaits the mother we saw in the school. Does she know the fate of her child? It is not for his return that she watches with eagerness for the opening of the wicket. Her father-in-law has been for a long time a recipient of Michizané's bounties, but since his banishment, circumstances have forced her husband to follow the service of the enemy of his family's benefactor. He himself could not be untrue to his own cruel master; but his son could serve the cause of the grandsire's lord. As one acquainted with the exile's family, it was he who had been entrusted with the task of identifying the boy's head. Now the day's — yea, the life's — hard work is done, he returns home and as he crosses its threshold, he accosts his wife, saying: 'Rejoice, my wife, our darling son has proved of service to his lord!'

'What an atrocious story!' I hear my readers exclaim. 'Parents deliberately sacrificing their own innocent child to save the life of another man's!' But this child was a conscious and willing victim: it is a story of vicarious death — as significant as, and not more revolting than, the story of Abraham's intended sacrifice of Isaac. In both cases was obedience to the call of duty, utter submission to the command of a higher voice, whether given by a visible or an invisible angel, or heard by an outward or an inward ear; but I abstain from preaching.

The individualism of the West, which recognizes separate interests for father and son, husband and wife, necessarily brings into strong relief the duties owed by one to the other; but Bushido held that the interest of the family and of the members thereof is intact — one and inseparable. This interest it bound up with affection — natural, instinctive, irresistible; hence, if we die for one we love with natural love (which animals themselves possess), what is that? 'For if ye love them that love you, what reward have ye? Do not even the publicans the same?'

In his great history, Sanyo relates in touching language the heart struggle of Shigemori concerning his father's rebellious conduct. 'If I be loyal, my father must be undone; if I obey my father, my duty to my sovereign must go amiss.' Poor Shigemori! We see him afterward praying with all his soul that kind Heaven may visit him with death, that he may be released from this world where it is hard for purity and righteousness to dwell.

Many a Shigemori has his heart torn by the conflict between duty and affection. Indeed, neither Shakespeare nor the Old Testament itself contains an adequate rendering of *ko*, our conception of filial piety, and yet in such conflicts Bushido never wavered in its choice of loyalty. Women, too, encouraged their offspring to sacrifice all for the king. Even as resolute as Widow Windham and

her illustrious consort, the samurai matron stood ready to give up her boys for the cause of loyalty.

Since Bushido, like Aristotle and some modern sociologists, conceived the state as antedating the individual – the latter being born into the former as part and parcel thereof – he must live and die for it or for the incumbent of its legitimate authority. Readers of *Crito* will remember the argument with which Socrates represents the laws of the city as pleading with him on the subject of his escape. Among others he makes them (the laws or the state) say: 'Since you were begotten and nurtured and educated under us, dare you once to say you are not our offspring and servant, you and your fathers before you?' These are words which do not impress us as any thing extraordinary; for the same thing has long been on the lips of Bushido, with this modification, that the laws and the state were represented with us by a personal being. Loyalty is an ethical outcome of this political theory.

I am not entirely ignorant of Mr. Spencer's view according to which political obedience – loyalty – is accredited with only a transitional function.[17] It may be so. Sufficient unto the day is the virtue thereof. We may complacently repeat it, especially as we believe that day to be a long space of time, during which, so our national anthem says, 'tiny pebbles grow into mighty rocks draped with moss.'

Political subordination, Mr. Spencer predicts, will give place to loyalty, to the dictates of conscience. Suppose his induction is realized – will loyalty and its concomitant instinct of reverence disappear forever? We transfer our allegiance from one master to another, without being unfaithful to either: from being subjects of a ruler that wields the temporal sceptre we become servants of the monarch who sits enthroned in the penetralia of our hearts. A few years ago a very stupid controversy, started by the misguided disciples of Spencer, made havoc among the reading class of Japan. In their zeal to uphold the claim of the throne to undivided loyalty, they charged Christians with treasonable propensity in that they avow fidelity to their Lord and Master. They arrayed forth sophistical arguments without the wit of Sophists, and scholastic tortuosities minus the niceties of the Schoolmen. Little did they know that we can, in a sense, 'serve two masters without holding to the one or despising the other,' 'rendering unto Caesar the things that are Caesar's and unto God the things that are God's.'

Did not Socrates, all the while he unflinchingly refused to concede one iota of loyalty to his *daemon*, obey with equal fidelity and equanimity the command of his earthly master, the State? His conscience he followed, alive; his country he served, dying. Alack the day when a state grows so powerful as to demand of its citizens the dictates of their conscience!

Bushido did not require us to make our conscience the slave of any lord or king. Thomas Mowbray was a veritable spokesman for us when he said:

> '*Myself I throw, dread sovereign, at thy foot.*
> *My life thou shall command, but not my shame.*
> *The one my duty owes; but my fair name,*
> *Despite of death, that lives upon my grave,*
> *To dark dishonour's use, thou shall not have.*'

A man who sacrificed his own conscience to the capricious will or freak or fancy of a sovereign was accorded a low place in the estimate of the Precepts. Such a one was despised as *nei-shin*, a cringeling, who makes court by unscrupulous fawning, or as *chô-shin*, a favourite who steals his master's affections by means of servile compliance; these two species of subjects corresponding exactly to those which Iago describes – the one, a duteous and knee-crooking knave, doting on his own obsequious bondage, wearing out his time much like his master's ass; the other trimming in forms and visages of duty, keeping yet his heart attending on himself. When a subject differed from his master, the loyal path for him to pursue was to use every available means to persuade him of his error, as Kent did to King Lear. Failing in this, let the master deal with him as he wills. In cases of this kind, it was quite a usual course for the samurai to make the last appeal to the intelligence and conscience of his lord by demonstrating the sincerity of his words with the shedding of his own blood.

Life being regarded as the means whereby to serve his master, and its ideal being set upon honour, the whole education and training of a samurai were conducted accordingly.

CHAPTER TEN

The Education and Traning of a Samurai

The first point to observe in knightly pedagogics was to build up character, leaving in the shade the subtler faculties of prudence, intelligence and dialectics. We have seen the important part aesthetic accomplishments played in his education. Indispensable as they were to a man of culture, they were accessories rather than essentials of samurai training. Intellectual superiority was, of course, esteemed; but the word *Chi*, which was employed to denote intellectuality, meant wisdom in the first instance and gave knowledge only a very subordinate place. The tripod which supported the framework of Bushido was said to be *Chi, Jin, Yu*, respectively, Wisdom, Benevolence, and Courage. A samurai was essentially a man of action. Science was without the pale of his activity. He took advantage of it in so far as it concerned his profession of arms. Religion and theology were relegated to the priests; he concerned himself with them in so far as they helped to nourish courage. Like an English poet the samurai believed ''tis not the creed that saves the man; but it is the man that justifies the creed.' Philosophy and literature formed the chief part of his intellectual training; but even in the pursuit of these, it was not objective truth that he strove after — literature was pursued mainly as a pastime, and philosophy as a practical aid in the formation of character, if not for the exposition of some military or political problem.

From what has been said, it will not be surprising to note that the curriculum of studies, according to the pedagogics of Bushido, consisted mainly of the following: fencing, archery, *jiujutsu*[18] or *yawara*, horsemanship, the use of the spear, tactics, calligraphy, ethics, literature, and history. Of these, *jiujutsu* and calligraphy may require a few words of explanation. Great stress was laid on good writing, probably because our logograms, partaking as they do of the nature of pictures, possess artistic value, and also because chirography was accepted as indicative of one's personal character. *Jiujutsu* may be briefly defined as an application of anatomical knowledge to the purpose of offence or defence. It differs from wrestling, in that it does not depend upon muscular strength. It differs from other forms of attack in that it uses no weapons. Its feat consists in clutching or striking such part of the enemy's body as will make him numb and incapable of resistance. Its object is not to kill, but to incapacitate one for action for the time being.

A subject of study which one would expect to find in military education and which is rather conspicuous by its absence in the Bushido course of instruction, is mathematics. This, however, can be readily explained in part by the fact that feudal warfare was not carried on with scientific precision. Not only that, but the whole training of the samurai was unfavourable to fostering numerical notions.

Chivalry is uneconomical: it boasts of penury. It says with Ventidius that 'ambition, the soldier's virtue, rather makes choice of loss, than gain which darkens him.' Don Quixote takes more pride in his rusty spear and skin-and-bone horse than in gold and lands, and a samurai is in hearty sympathy with his exaggerated confrère of La Mancha. He disdains money itself – the art of making or hoarding it. It was to him veritably filthy lucre. The hackneyed expression to describe the decadence of an age was 'that the civilians loved money and the soldiers feared death.' Niggardliness of gold and of life excited as much disapprobation as their lavish use was panegyrized. 'Less than all things,' says a current precept, 'men must grudge money: it is by riches that wisdom is hindered.' Hence children were brought up with utter disregard of economy. It was considered bad taste to speak of it, and ignorance of the value of different coins was a token of good breeding. Knowledge of numbers was indispensable in the mustering of forces as well as in distribution of benefices and fiefs; but the counting of money was left to meaner hands. In many feudatories, public finance was administered by a lower kind of samurai or by priests. Every thinking bushi knew well enough that money formed the sinews of war; but he did not think of raising the appreciation of money to a virtue. It is true that thrift was enjoined by Bushido, but not for economical reasons so much as for the exercise of abstinence. Luxury was thought the greatest menace to manhood and severest simplicity of living was required of the warrior class, sumptuary laws being enforced in many of the clans.

We read that in ancient Rome the farmers of revenue and other financial agents were gradually raised to the rank of knights, the State thereby showing its appreciation of their service and of the importance of money itself. How closely this is connected with the luxury and avarice of the Romans may be imagined. Not so with the Precepts of Knighthood. It persisted in systematically regarding finance as something low – low as compared with moral and intellectual vocations.

Money and the love of it being thus diligently ignored, Bushido itself could long remain free from a thousand and one evils of which money is the root. This is sufficient reason for the fact that our public men have long been free from corruption; but alas! how fast plutocracy is making its way in our time and generation.

The mental discipline which would nowadays be chiefly aided by the study of mathematics, was supplied by literary exegesis and deontological discussions. Very few abstract subjects troubled the mind of the young, the chief aim of their education being, as I have said, decision of character. People whose minds were simply stored with information found no great admirers. Of the three services of studies that Bacon gives – for delight, ornament, and ability – Bushido had decided preference for the last, where their use was 'in judgment and the disposition of business.' Whether it was for the disposition of public business or for the exercise of self-control, it was with a practical end in view that education was conducted. 'Learning without thought,' said Confucius, 'is labour lost; thought without learning is perilous.'

When character and not intelligence, when the soul and not the head, is chosen by a teacher for the material to work upon and to develop, his vocation partakes of a sacred character. 'It is the parent who has borne me: it is the teacher who makes me man.' With this idea, therefore, the esteem in which one's preceptor was held was very high. A man to evoke such confidence and respect from the young, must necessarily be endowed with superior personality, without lacking erudition. He was a father to the fatherless, and an adviser to the erring. 'Thy father and thy mother' – so runs our maxim – 'are like heaven and earth; thy teacher and thy lord are like the sun and moon.'

The present system of paying for every sort of service was not in vogue among the adherents of Bushido. It believed in a service which can be rendered only without money and without price. Spiritual service, be it of priest or teacher, was not to be repaid in gold or silver, not because it was valueless but because it was invaluable. Here the non-arithmetical honour-instinct of Bushido taught a truer lesson than modern Political Economy; for wages and salaries can be paid only for services whose results are definite, tangible, and measurable, whereas the best service done in education – namely, in soul development (and this includes the services of a pastor) – is not definite, tangible, or measurable. Being immeasurable, money, the ostensible measure of value, is of inadequate use. Usage sanctioned that pupils brought to their teachers money or goods at different seasons of the year; but these were not payments but offerings, which indeed were welcome to the recipients as they were usually men of stern calibre, boasting of honourable penury, too dignified to work with their hands and too proud to beg. They were grave personifications of high spirits undaunted by adversity. They were an embodiment of what was considered as an end of all learning, and were thus a living example of that discipline of disciplines, self-control, which was universally required of samurai.

CHAPTER ELEVEN

Self-Control

The discipline of fortitude on the one hand, inculcating endurance without a groan, and the teaching of politeness on the other, requiring us not to mar the pleasure or serenity of another by expressions of our own sorrow or pain, combined to engender a turn of mind, and eventually to confirm it into a national trait of apparent stoicism. I say apparent stoicism, because I do not believe that true stoicism can ever become the characteristic of a whole nation, and also because some of our national manners and customs may seem to a foreign observer hard-hearted. Yet we are really as susceptible to tender emotion as any race under the sky.

I am inclined to think that in one sense we have to feel more than others – yes, doubly more – since the very attempt to restrain natural promptings entails suffering. Imagine boys – and girls, too – brought up not to resort to the shedding of a tear or the uttering of a groan for the relief of their feelings – and there is a physiological problem whether such effort steels their nerves or makes them more sensitive.

It was considered unmanly for a samurai to betray his emotions on his face. 'He shows no sign of joy or anger,' was a phrase used, in describing a great character. The most natural affections were kept under control. A father could embrace his son only at the expense of his dignity; a husband would not kiss his wife – no, not in the presence of other people, whatever he might do in

private! There may be some truth in the remark of a witty youth when he said, 'American husbands kiss their wives in public and beat them in private; Japanese husbands beat theirs in public and kiss them in private.'

Calmness of behaviour, composure of mind, should not be disturbed by passion of any kind. I remember when, during the late war with China, a regiment left a certain town, a large concourse of people flocked to the station to bid farewell to the general and his army. On this occasion an American resident resorted to the place, expecting to witness loud demonstrations, as the nation itself was highly excited and there were fathers, mothers, wives, and sweethearts of the soldiers in the crowd. The American was strangely disappointed; for as the whistle blew and the train began to move, the hats of thousands of people were silently taken off and their heads bowed in reverential farewell; no waving of handkerchiefs, no word uttered, but deep silence in which only an attentive ear could catch a few broken sobs. In domestic life, too, I know of a father who spent whole nights listening to the breathing of a sick child, standing behind the door that he might not be caught in such an act of parental weakness! I know of a mother who, in her last moments, refrained from sending for her son, that he might not be disturbed in his studies. Our history and everyday life are replete with examples of heroic matrons who can well bear comparison with some of the most touching pages of Plutarch.

It is the same discipline of self-restraint which is accountable for the absence of more frequent revivals in the Christian churches of Japan. When a man or woman feels his or her soul stirred, the first instinct is quietly to suppress the manifestation of it. In rare instances is the tongue set free by an irresistible spirit, when we have eloquence of sincerity and fervour. It is putting a premium upon a breach of the third commandment to encourage speaking lightly of spiritual experience. It is truly jarring to Japanese ears to hear the most sacred words, the most secret heart experiences, thrown out in promiscuous audiences. 'Dost thou feel the soil of thy soul stirred with tender thoughts? It is time for seeds to sprout. Disturb it not with speech; but let it work alone in quietness and secrecy,' writes a young samurai in his diary.

To give in so many articulate words one's inmost thoughts and feelings – notably the religious – is taken among us as an unmistakable sign that they are neither very profound nor very sincere. 'Only a pomegranate is he' – so runs a popular saying 'who, when he gapes his mouth, displays the contents of his heart.'

It is not altogether perverseness of oriental minds that the instant our emotions are moved, we try to guard our lips in order to hide them. Speech is very often with us, as the Frenchman defines it, 'the art of concealing thought.'

Call upon a Japanese friend in time of deepest affliction and he will invariably receive you laughing, with red eyes or moist cheeks. At first you may think him hysterical. Press him for explanation and you will get a few broken commonplaces – 'Human life has sorrow'; 'They who meet must part'; 'He that is born must die'; 'It is foolish to count the years of a child that is gone, but a woman's heart will indulge in follies'; and the like. So the noble words of a noble Hohenzollern – '*Lerne zu leiden ohne klagen*'[19] – had found many responsive minds among us long before they were uttered.

Indeed, the Japanese have recourse to risibility whenever the frailties of human nature are put to the severest test. I think we possess a better reason than Democritus himself for our Abderian tendency, for laughter with us oftenest veils an effort to regain balance of temper when disturbed by any untoward circumstance. It is a counterpoise of sorrow or rage.

The suppression of feelings being thus steadily insisted upon, they find their safety-valve in poetical aphorisms. A poet of the tenth century writes 'In Japan and China as well, humanity, when moved by sorrow, tells its bitter grief in verse.' Another who tries to console her broken heart by fancying her departed child absent on his wonted chase after the dragon-fly hums,

> '*How far to-day in chase, I wonder,*
> *Has gone my hunter of the dragon-fly!*'

I refrain from quoting other examples, for I know I could do only scant justice to the pearly gems of our literature, were I to render into a foreign tongue the thoughts which were wrung drop by drop from bleeding hearts and threaded into beads of rarest value. I hope I have in a measure shown that inner working of our minds which often presents an appearance of callousness or of an hysterical mixture of laughter and dejection, and whose sanity is sometimes called in question.

It has also been suggested that our endurance of pain and indifference to death are due to less sensitive nerves. This is plausible as far as it goes. The next question is, why are our nerves less tightly strung? It may be our climate is not so stimulating as the American. It may be our monarchical form of government does not excite us so much as the Republic does the Frenchman. It may be that we do not read *Sartor Resartus* so zealously as the Englishman. Personally, I believe it was our very excitability and sensitiveness which made it a necessity to recognize and enforce constant self-repression; but whatever may be the explanation, without taking into account long years of discipline in self-control, none can be correct.

Discipline in self-control can easily go too far. It can well repress the genial current of the soul. It can force pliant natures into distortions and monstrosities. It can beget bigotry, breed hypocrisy, or hebetate affections. Be a virtue never so noble, it has its counterpart and counterfeit. We must recognize in each virtue its own positive excellence and follow its positive ideal, and the ideal of self-restraint is to keep the mind level – as our expression is – or, to borrow a Greek term, attain the state of euthymia, which Democritus called the highest good.

The acme and pitch of self-control is reached and best illustrated in the first of the two institutions which we shall now bring to view, namely, the institutions of suicide and redress.

CHAPTER TWELVE

The Institutions of
Suicide and Redress

Of these two institutions (the former known as *hara-kiri* and the latter as *kataki-uchi*), many foreign writers have treated more or less fully.

To begin with suicide, let me state that I confine my observations only to *seppuku* or *kappuku*, popularly known as *hara-kiri* – which means self-immolation by disembowelment. 'Ripping the abdomen? How absurd!' – so cry those to whom the name is new. Absurdly odd as it may sound at first to foreign ears, it cannot be so very foreign to students of Shakespeare, who puts these words in Brutus's mouth – 'Thy [Caesar's] spirit walks abroad and turns our swords into our proper entrails.' Listen to a modern English poet[20] who, in his *Light of Asia*, speaks of a sword piercing the bowels of a queen; none blames him for bad English or breach of modesty. Or, to take still another example, look at Guercino's painting of Cato's death in the Palazzo Rossa, in Genoa. Whoever has read the swan-song which Addison makes Cato sing, will not jeer at the sword half-buried in his abdomen. In our minds this mode of death is associated with instances of noblest deeds and of most touching pathos, so that nothing repugnant, much less ludicrous, mars our conception of it. So wonderful is the transforming power of virtue, of greatness, of tenderness, that the vilest form of death assumes a sublimity and becomes a symbol of new life, or else the sign which Constantine beheld would not conquer the world!

Not for extraneous associations only does *seppuku* lose in our mind any taint of absurdity; for the choice of this particular part of the body to operate upon, was based on an old anatomical belief as to the seat of the soul and of the affections. When Moses wrote of Joseph's 'bowels yearning upon his brother,' or David prayed the Lord not to forget his bowels, or when Isaiah, Jeremiah, and other inspired men of old spoke of the 'sounding' or the 'troubling' of bowels, they all and each endorsed the belief prevalent among the Japanese that in the abdomen was enshrined the soul. The Semites habitually spoke of the liver and kidneys and surrounding fat as the seat of emotion and of life. The term '*hara*' was more comprehensive than the Greek *phren* or *thumos*, and the Japanese and Hellenese alike thought the spirit of man to dwell somewhere in that region. Such a notion is by no means confined to the peoples of antiquity. The French, in spite of the theory propounded by one of their most distinguished philosophers, Descartes, that the soul is located in the pineal gland, still insist in using the term *ventre* in a sense which, if anatomically too vague, is nevertheless physiologically significant. Similarly, *entrailles* stands in their language for affection and compassion. Nor is such a belief mere superstition, being more scientific than the general idea of making the heart the centre of the feelings. Without asking a friar, the Japanese knew better than Romeo 'in what vile part of this anatomy one's name did lodge.' Modern neurologists speak of the abdominal and pelvic brains, denoting thereby sympathetic nerve centres in those parts which are strongly affected by any psychical action. This view of mental physiology once admitted, the syllogism of *seppuku* is easy to construct. 'I will open the seat of my soul and show you how it fares with it. See for yourself whether it is polluted or clean.'

I do not wish to be understood as asserting religious or even moral justification of suicide, but the high estimate placed upon honour was ample excuse with many for taking one's own life. How many acquiesced in the sentiment expressed by Garth,

'When honour's lost, 't is a relief to die;
Death's but a sure retreat from infamy,'

and have smilingly surrendered their souls to oblivion! Death involving a question of honour, was accepted in Bushido as a key to the solution of many complex problems, so that to an ambitious samurai a natural departure from life seemed a rather tame affair and a consummation not devoutly to be wished for. I dare say that many good Christians, if only they are honest enough, will confess the fascination of, if not positive admiration for, the sublime composure with which Cato, Brutus, Petronius, and a host of other ancient worthies terminated their own earthly existence. Is it too bold to hint that the death of the first of the philosophers was partly suicidal? When we are told so minutely by his pupils how their master willingly submitted to the mandate of the state – which he knew was morally mistaken – in spite of the possibilities of escape, and how he took the cup of hemlock in his own hand, even offering libation from its deadly contents, do we not discern, in his whole proceeding and demeanour, an act of self-immolation? No physical compulsion here, as in ordinary cases of execution. True, the verdict of the judges was compulsory: it said, 'Thou shalt die – and that by thine own hand.' If suicide meant no more than dying by one's own hand, Socrates was a clear case of suicide. But nobody would charge him with the crime; Plato, who was averse to it, would not call his master a suicide. Now my readers will understand that *seppuku* was not a mere suicidal process. It was an institution, legal and ceremonial. An invention of the middle ages, it was a process by which warriors could expiate their crimes, apologize for errors, escape from disgrace, redeem their friends, or prove their sincerity. When enforced as a legal punishment, it was practised with due ceremony. It was a refinement of self-destruction, and none could perform it without the utmost coolness of temper and composure of demeanour, and for these reasons it was particularly befitting the profession of bushi.

Antiquarian curiosity, if nothing else, would tempt me to give here a description of this obsolete ceremony; but seeing that such a description was made by a far abler writer, whose book is not much read nowadays, I am tempted to make

a somewhat lengthy quotation. Mitford, in his *Tales of Old Japan*, after giving a translation of a treatise on *seppuku* from a rare Japanese manuscript, goes on to describe an instance of such an execution of which he was an eye-witness:

> 'We (seven foreign representatives) were invited to follow the Japanese witnesses into the hondo or main hall of the temple, where the ceremony was to be performed. It was an imposing scene. A large hall with a high roof supported by dark pillars of wood. From the ceiling hung a profusion of those huge gilt lamps and ornaments peculiar to Buddhist temples. In front of the high altar, where the floor, covered with beautiful white mats, is raised some three or four inches from the ground, was laid a rug of scarlet felt. Tall candles placed at regular intervals gave out a dim mysterious light, just sufficient to let all the proceedings be seen. The seven Japanese took their places on the left of the raised floor, the seven foreigners on the right. No other person was present.
>
> 'After the interval of a few minutes of anxious suspense, Taki Zenzaburo, a stalwart man thirty-two years of age, with a noble air, walked into the hall attired in his dress of ceremony, with the peculiar hempen-cloth wings which are worn on great occasions. He was accompanied by a kaishaku and three officers, who wore the jimbaori or war surcoat with gold tissue facings. The word kaishaku, it should be observed, is one to which our word executioner is no equivalent term. The office is that of a gentleman; in many cases it is performed by a kinsman or friend of the condemned, and the relation between them is rather that of principal and second than that of victim and executioner. In this instance, the kaishaku was a pupil of Taki Zenzaburo, and was selected by friends of the latter from among their own number for his skill in swordsmanship.
>
> 'With the kaishaku on his left hand, Taki Zenzaburo advanced slowly toward the Japanese witnesses, and the two bowed before them, then drawing near to the foreigners they saluted us in the same way, perhaps even with more deference; in each case the salutation was ceremoniously returned. Slowly and with great dignity the condemned man mounted on to the raised floor, prostrated himself before the high altar twice, and seated[21] himself on the felt carpet with his back to the high altar, the kaishaku crouching on his left-hand side. One of the three attendant officers then came forward, bearing a stand of the kind used in the temple for

offerings, on which, wrapped in paper, lay the wakizashi, *the short sword or dirk of the Japanese, nine inches and a half in length, with a point and an edge as sharp as a razor's. This he handed, prostrating himself, to the condemned man, who received it reverently raising it to his head with both hands, and placed it in front of himself.*

'*After another profound obeisance, Taki Zenzaburo, in a voice which betrayed just so much emotion and hesitation as might be expected from a man who is making a painful confession, but with no sign of either in his face or manner, spoke as follows:* –

'"*I, and I alone, unwarrantably gave the order to fire on the foreigners at Kobe, and again as they tried to escape. For this crime I disembowel myself, and I beg you who are present to do me the honour of witnessing the act.*"

'*Bowing once more, the speaker allowed his upper garments to slip down to his girdle, and remained naked to the waist. Carefully, according to custom, he tucked his sleeves under his knees to prevent himself from falling backward; for a noble Japanese gentleman should die falling forwards. Deliberately, with a steady hand he took the dirk that lay before him; he looked at it wistfully, almost affectionately; for a moment he seemed to collect his thoughts for the last time, and then stabbing himself deeply below the waist in the left-hand side, he drew the dirk slowly across to his right side, and turning it in the wound, gave a slight cut upwards. During this sickeningly painful operation he never moved a muscle of his face. When he drew out the dirk, he leaned forward and stretched out his neck; an expression of pain for the first time crossed his face, but he uttered no sound. At that moment the* kaishaku, *who, still crouching by his side, had been keenly watching his every movement, sprang to his feet, poised his sword for a second in the air; there was a flash, a heavy, ugly thud, a crashing fall; with one blow the head had been severed from the body.*

'*A dead silence followed, broken only by the hideous noise of the blood throbbing out of the inert heap before us, which but a moment before had been a brave and chivalrous man. It was horrible.*

'*The* kaishaku *made a low bow, wiped his sword with a piece of paper which he had ready for the purpose, and retired from the raised floor; and the stained dirk was solemnly borne away, a bloody proof of the execution.*

'*The two representatives of the Mikado then left their places, and crossing over to where the foreign witnesses sat, called to us to witness that the sentence of death upon Taki Zenzaburo had been faithfully carried out. The ceremony being at an end, we left the temple.'*

The glorification of *seppuku* offered, naturally enough, no small temptation to its unwarranted committal. For causes entirely incompatible with reason, or for reasons entirely undeserving of death, hot-headed youths rushed into it as insects fly into fire; mixed and dubious motives drove more samurai to this deed than nuns into convent gates. Life was cheap – cheap as reckoned by the popular standard of honour. The saddest feature was that honour, which was always in the *agio*, so to speak, was not always solid gold, but alloyed with baser metals. No one circle in the Inferno will boast of greater density of Japanese population than the seventh, to which Dante consigns all victims of self-destruction!

And yet, for a true samurai to hasten death or to court it, was alike cowardice. A typical fighter, when he lost battle after battle and was pursued from plain to hill and from bush to cavern, found himself hungry and alone in the dark hollow of a tree, his sword blunt with use, his bow broken and arrows exhausted – did not the noblest of the Romans fall upon his own sword in Philippi under like circumstances? – deemed it cowardly to die, but, with a fortitude approaching a Christian martyr's, cheered himself with an impromptu verse:

'Come! evermore come,
Ye dread sorrows and pains!
And heap on my burden'd back;
That I not one test may lack
Of what strength in me remains!'

This, then, was the Bushido teaching – Bear and face all calamities and adversities with patience and a pure conscience; for, as Mencius[22] taught, 'When Heaven is about to confer a great office on anyone, it first exercises his mind with suffering and his sinews and bones with toil; it exposes his body to hunger and subjects him to extreme poverty: and it confounds his undertakings. In all these ways it stimulates his mind, hardens his nature, and supplies his incompetencies.' True honour lies in fulfilling Heaven's decree and no death incurred in so doing is ignominious, whereas, death to avoid what Heaven has in store is cowardly indeed! In that quaint book of Sir Thomas Browne's, *Religio Medici*, there is an exact English equivalent for what is repeatedly taught in our Precepts. Let me quote it: 'It is a brave act of valour to contemn death, but where life is more terrible than death, it is then the truest valour to dare to live.' A renowned priest of the seventeenth century satirically observed – 'Talk as he may, a samurai who ne'er has died is apt in decisive moments to flee or hide.' Again – 'Him who once has died in the bottom of his breast, no spears of Sanada nor all the arrows of Tametomo can pierce.' How near we come to the portals of the temple whose Builder taught, 'He that loseth his life for my sake shall find it'! These are but a few of the numerous examples that tend to confirm the moral identity of

the human species, notwithstanding an attempt so assiduously made to render the distinction between Christian and Pagan as great as possible.

We have thus seen that the Bushido institution of suicide was neither so irrational nor barbarous as its abuse strikes us at first sight. We will now see whether its sister institution of Redress – or call it Revenge, if you will – has its mitigating features. I hope I can dispose of this question in a few words, since a similar institution, or call it custom, if that suits you better, prevailed among all peoples and has not yet become entirely obsolete, as attested by the continuance of duelling and lynching. Why, has not an American captain recently challenged Esterhazy, that the wrongs of Dreyfus be avenged? Among a savage tribe which has no marriage, adultery is not a sin, and only the jealousy of a lover protects a woman from abuse; so in a time which has no criminal court, murder is not a crime, and only the vigilant vengeance of the victim's people preserves social order. 'What is the most beautiful thing on earth?' said Osiris to Horus. The reply was, 'To avenge a parent's wrongs,' to which a Japanese would have added 'and a master's.'

In revenge there is something which satisfies one's sense of justice. The avenger reasons: 'My good father did not deserve death. He who killed him did great evil. My father, if he were alive, would not tolerate a deed like this: Heaven itself hates wrongdoing. It is the will of my father; it is the will of Heaven that the evil-doer cease from his work. He must perish by my hand; because he shed my father's blood, I, who am his flesh and blood, must shed the murderer's. The same Heaven shall not shelter him and me.' The ratiocination is simple and childish (though we know Hamlet did not reason much more deeply); nevertheless it shows an innate sense of exact balance and equal justice. 'An eye for an eye, a tooth for a tooth.' Our sense of revenge is as exact as our mathematical faculty, and until both terms of the equation are satisfied we cannot get over the sense of something left undone.

In Judaism, which believed in a jealous God, or in Greek mythology, which provided a Nemesis, vengeance may be left to superhuman agencies; but common sense furnished Bushido with the institution of redress as a kind of ethical court of equity, where people could take cases not to be judged in accordance with ordinary law. The master of the forty-seven Ronins was condemned to death;

he had no court of higher instance to appeal to; his faithful retainers addressed themselves to vengeance, the only Supreme Court existing; they in their turn were condemned by common law – but the popular instinct passed a different judgment, and hence their memory is still kept as green and fragrant as are their graves at Sengakuji to this day.

Though Lâo-tse taught to recompense injury with kindness, the voice of Confucius was very much louder, which taught that injury must be recompensed with justice – and yet revenge was justified only when it was undertaken in behalf of our superiors and benefactors. One's own wrongs, including injuries done to wife and children, were to be borne and forgiven. A samurai could therefore fully sympathize with Hannibal's oath to avenge his country's wrongs, but he scorns James Hamilton for wearing in his girdle a handful of earth from his wife's grave, as an eternal incentive to avenge her wrongs on the Regent Murray.

Both of these institutions of suicide and redress lost their *raison d'être* at the promulgation of the Criminal Code. No more do we hear of romantic adventures of a fair maiden as she tracks in disguise the murderer of her parent. No more can we witness tragedies of family vendetta enacted. The knight errantry of Miyamoto Musashi is now a tale of the past. The well-ordered police spies out the criminal for the injured party and the law metes out justice. The whole state and society will see that wrong is righted. The sense of justice satisfied, there is no need of *kataki-uchi*. If this had meant that 'hunger of the heart which feeds upon the hope of glutting that hunger with the life blood of the victim,' as a New England divine has described it, a few paragraphs in the Criminal Code would not so entirely have made an end of it.

As to *seppuku*, though it too has no existence *de jure*, we still hear of it from time to time, and shall continue to hear, I am afraid, as long as the past is remembered. Many painless and time-saving methods of self-immolation will come in vogue, as its votaries are increasing with fearful rapidity throughout the world; but Professor Morselli will have to concede to *seppuku* an aristocratic position among them. He maintains that 'when suicide is accomplished by very painful means or at the cost of prolonged agony, in ninety-nine cases out of a hundred, it may be assigned as the act of a mind disordered by fanaticism, by

madness, or by morbid excitement.'[23] But a normal *seppuku* does not savour of fanaticism, or madness or excitement, utmost *sang froid* being necessary to its successful accomplishment. Of the two kinds into which Dr. Strahan[24] divides suicide, the Rational or Quasi, and the Irrational or True, *seppuku* is the best example of the former type.

From these bloody institutions, as well as from the general tenor of Bushido, it is easy to infer that the sword played an important part in social discipline and life. The saying passed as an axiom which called the sword the soul of the samurai.

CHAPTER THIRTEEN

The Sword,
the Soul of the Samurai

Bushido made the sword its emblem of power and prowess. When Mahomet proclaimed that 'the sword is the key of Heaven and of Hell,' he only echoed a Japanese sentiment. Very early the samurai boy learned to wield it. It was a momentous occasion for him when at the age of five he was apparelled in the paraphernalia of samurai costume, placed upon a *go*-board[25] and initiated into the rights of the military profession, by having thrust into his girdle a real sword instead of the toy dirk with which he had been playing. After this first ceremony of *adoptio per arma*, he was no more to be seen outside his father's gates without this badge of his status, even though it was usually substituted for everyday wear by a gilded wooden dirk. Not many years pass before he wears constantly the genuine steel, though blunt, and then the sham arms are thrown aside and with enjoyment keener than his newly acquired blades, he marches out to try their edge on wood and stone. When he reaches man's estate, at the age of fifteen, being given independence of action, he can now pride himself upon the possession of arms sharp enough for any work. The very possession of the dangerous instrument imparts to him a feeling and an air of self-respect and responsibility. 'He beareth not the sword in vain.' What he carries in his belt is a symbol of what he carries in his mind and heart – loyalty and honour. The two swords, the longer and the shorter – called respectively *daito* and *shoto* or *katana* and *wakizashi* – never leave his side. When at home, they grace the most conspicuous place in the study or parlour; by night they guard his pillow within easy reach of his hand. Constant companions, they are beloved, and proper names of endearment given them. Being venerated, they are well-nigh worshipped. The Father of History has recorded as a curious piece of information that the Scythians sacrificed to an iron scimitar. Many a temple and many a family in Japan hoards a sword as an object of adoration. Even the commonest dirk has due respect paid to it. Any insult to it is tantamount to personal affront. Woe to him who carelessly steps over a weapon lying on the floor!

So precious an object cannot long escape the notice and the skill of artists nor the vanity of its owner, especially in times of peace, when it is worn with no more use than a crosier by a bishop or a sceptre by a king. Sharkskin and finest silk for hilt, silver and gold for guard, lacquer of varied hues for scabbard, robbed the deadliest weapon of half its terror; but these appurtenances are playthings compared with the blade itself.

The swordsmith was not a mere artisan but an inspired artist and his workshop a sanctuary. Daily he commenced his craft with prayer and purification, or, as the phrase was, 'he committed his soul and spirit into the forging and tempering of the steel.' Every swing of the sledge, every plunge into water, every friction on the grindstone, was a religious act of no slight import. Was it the spirit of the master or of his tutelary god that cast a formidable spell over our sword? Perfect as a work of art, setting at defiance its Toledo and Damascus rivals, there was more than art could impart. Its cold blade, collecting on its surface the moment it is drawn the vapour of the atmosphere; its immaculate texture, flashing light of bluish hue; its matchless edge, upon which histories and possibilities hang; the curve of its back, uniting exquisite grace with utmost strength – all these thrill us with mixed feelings of power and beauty, of awe and terror. Harmless were its mission, if it only remained a thing of beauty and joy! But, ever within reach of the hand, it presented no small temptation for abuse. Too often did the blade flash forth from its peaceful sheath. The abuse sometimes went so far as to try the acquired steel on some harmless creature's neck.

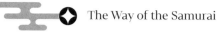

The question that concerns us most is, however – Did Bushido justify the promiscuous use of the weapon? The answer is unequivocally, no! As it laid great stress on its proper use, so did it denounce and abhor its misuse. A dastard or a braggart was he who brandished his weapon on undeserved occasions. A self-possessed man knows the right time to use it, and such times come but rarely. Let us listen to the late Count Katsu, who passed through one of the most turbulent times of our history, when assassinations, suicides, and other sanguinary practices were the order of the day. Endowed as he once was with almost dictatorial powers, chosen repeatedly as an object of assassination, he never tarnished his sword with blood. In relating some of his reminiscences to a friend he says, in a quaint, plebeian way peculiar to him: 'I have a great dislike for killing people and so I haven't killed one single man. I have released those whose heads should have been chopped off. A friend said to me one day, "You don't kill enough. Don't you eat pepper and egg-plants?" Well, some people are no better! But you see that fellow was slain himself. My escape may be due to my dislike of killing. I had the hilt of my sword so tightly fastened to the scabbard that it was hard to draw the blade. I made up my mind that though they cut me, I would not cut. Yes, yes! some people are truly like fleas and mosquitoes and they bite – but what does their biting amount to? It itches a little, that's all; it won't endanger life.' These are the words of one whose Bushido training was tried in the fiery furnace of adversity and triumph. The popular apothegm – 'To be beaten is to conquer,' meaning true conquest consists in not opposing a riotous foe; and 'The best won victory is that obtained without shedding of blood,' and others of similar import – will show that after all the ultimate ideal of knighthood was peace.

It was a great pity that this high ideal was left exclusively to priests and moralists to preach, while the samurai went on practising and extolling martial traits. In this they went so far as to tinge the ideals of womanhood with Amazonian character. Here we may profitably devote a few paragraphs to the subject of the training and position of woman.

CHAPTER FOURTEEN

The Training and Position of Woman

The female half of our species has sometimes been called the paragon of paradoxes, because the intuitive working of its mind is beyond the comprehension of men's 'arithmetical understanding.' The Chinese ideogram denoting 'the mysterious,' 'the unknowable,' consists of two parts, one meaning 'young' and the other 'woman,' because the physical charms and delicate thoughts of the fair sex are above the coarse mental calibre of our sex to explain.

In the Bushido ideal of woman, however, there is little mystery and only a seeming paradox. I have said that it was Amazonian, but that is only half the truth. Ideographically the Chinese represent wife by a woman holding a broom – certainly not to brandish it offensively or defensively against her conjugal ally, neither for witchcraft, but for the more harmless uses for which the besom was first invented – the idea involved being thus not less homely than the etymological derivation of the English wife (weaver) and daughter (*duhitar*, milkmaid). Without confining the sphere of woman's activity to *Küche, Kirche, Kinder*,[26] as the present German Kaiser is said to do, the Bushido ideal of womanhood was pre-eminently domestic. These seeming contradictions – domesticity and Amazonian traits – are not inconsistent with the Precepts of Knighthood, as we shall see.

Bushido being a teaching primarily intended for the masculine sex, the virtues it prized in woman were naturally far from being distinctly feminine. Winckelmann remarks that 'the supreme beauty of Greek art is rather male than female,' and Lecky adds that it was true in the moral conception of the Greeks as in their art. Bushido similarly praised those women most 'who emancipated themselves from the frailty of their sex and displayed an heroic fortitude worthy of the strongest and the bravest of men.'[27] Young girls, therefore, were trained to repress their feelings, to indurate their nerves, to manipulate weapons – especially the long-handled sword called *nagi-nata*, so as to be able to hold their own against unexpected odds. Yet the primary motive for exercise of this martial character was not for use in the field; it was twofold – personal and domestic. Woman owning no suzerain of her own, formed her own body-guard. With her weapon she guarded her personal sanctity with as much zeal as her husband did his master's. The domestic utility of her warlike training was in the education of her sons, as we shall see later.

Fencing and similar exercises, if rarely of practical use, were a wholesome counterbalance to the otherwise sedentary habits of women. But these exercises were not followed only for hygienic purposes. They could be turned into use in times of need. Girls, when they reached womanhood, were presented with dirks (*kai-ken*, pocket poniards), which might be directed to the bosom of their assailants, or, if advisable, to their own. The latter was very often the case; and yet I will not judge them severely. Even the Christian conscience with its horror of self-immolation, will not be harsh with them, seeing Pelagia and Dominina, two suicides, were canonized for their purity and piety. When a Japanese Virginia saw her chastity menaced, she did not wait for her father's dagger. Her own weapon lay always in her bosom. It was a disgrace to her not to know the proper way in which she had to perpetrate self-destruction. For example, little as she was taught in anatomy, she must know the exact spot to cut in her throat; she must know how to tie her lower limbs together with a belt so that, whatever the agonies of death might be, her corpse be found in utmost modesty with the limbs properly composed. Is not a caution like this worthy of the Christian Perpetua or the Vestal Cornelia? I would not put such an abrupt interrogation were it not for a misconception, based on our bathing customs and other trifles, that chastity is unknown among us.[28] On the contrary, chastity was a pre-eminent virtue of the samurai woman, held above life itself.

It would be unfair to give my readers an idea that masculinity alone was our highest ideal for woman. Far from it! Accomplishments and the gentler graces of life were required of them. Music, dancing, and literature were not neglected. Some of the finest verses in our literature were expressions of feminine sentiments; in fact, woman played an important role in the history of Japanese *belles-lettres*. Dancing was taught (I am speaking of samurai girls and not of *geisha*) only to smooth the angularity of their movements. Music was to regale the weary hours of their fathers and husbands; hence it was not for the technique, the art as such, that music was learned; for the ultimate object was purification of heart, since it was said that no harmony of sound is attainable without the player's heart being in harmony with itself. Here again we see the same idea prevailing which we notice in the training of youths — that accomplishments were ever kept subservient to moral worth. Just enough of music and dancing to add grace and brightness to life, but never to foster vanity and extravagance.

The accomplishments of our women were not acquired for show or social ascendancy. They were a home diversion; and if they shone in social parties, it was as the attributes of a hostess — in other words, as a part of the household contrivance for hospitality. Domesticity guided their education. It may be said that the accomplishments of the women of Old Japan, be they martial or pacific in character, were mainly intended for the home; and, however far they might roam, they never lost sight of the hearth as the centre. It was to maintain its honour and integrity that they slaved, drudged, and gave up their lives. Night and day, in tones at once firm and tender, brave and plaintive, they sang to their little nests. As daughter, woman sacrificed herself for her father, as wife for her husband, and as mother for her son. Thus from earliest youth she was taught to deny herself. Her life was not one of independence, but of dependent service. Man's helpmeet, if her presence is helpful she stays on the stage with him: if it hinders his work, she retires behind the curtain. Not infrequently does it happen that a youth becomes enamoured of a maiden who returns his love with equal ardour, but, when she realizes his interest in her makes him forgetful of his duties, disfigures her person that her attractions may cease. Adzuma, the

ideal wife in the minds of samurai girls, finds herself loved by a man who is conspiring against her husband. Upon pretence of joining in the guilty plot, she manages in the dark to take her husband's place, and the sword of the lover-assassin descends upon her own devoted head.

Woman's surrender of herself to the good of her husband, home, and family, was as willing and honourable as the man's self-surrender to the good of his lord and country. Self-renunciation, without which no life-enigma can be solved, was the key-note of the loyalty of man as well as of the domesticity of woman. She was no more the slave of man than was her husband of his liege-lord, and the part she played was recognized as *naijo*, 'the inner help.' In the ascending scale of service stood woman, who annihilated herself for man, that he might annihilate himself for the master, that he in turn might obey Heaven. I know the weakness of this teaching and that the superiority of Christianity is nowhere more manifested than here, in that it requires of each and every living soul direct responsibility to its Creator. Nevertheless, as far as the doctrine of service is concerned, Bushido was based on eternal truth.

My readers will not accuse me of undue prejudice in favour of slavish surrender of volition. I accept in a large measure the view advanced and defended with breadth of learning and profundity of thought by Hegel, that history is the unfolding and realization of freedom. The point I wish to make is that the whole teaching of Bushido was so thoroughly imbued with the spirit of self-sacrifice, that it was required not only of woman but of man. Hence, until the influence of its precepts is entirely done away with, our society will not realize the view rashly expressed by an American exponent of woman's rights, who exclaimed, 'May all the daughters of Japan rise in revolt against ancient customs!' Can such a revolt succeed? Will it improve the female status? Will the rights they gain by such a summary process repay the loss of that sweetness of disposition, that gentleness of manner, which are their present heritage? Was not the loss of domesticity on the part of Roman matrons followed by moral corruption too gross to mention? Can the American reformer assure us that a revolt of our daughters is the true course for their historical development to take? These are grave questions. Changes must and will come without revolts! In the meantime let us see whether the status of the fair sex under the Bushido regimen was really so bad as to justify a revolt.

Mr. Spencer tells us that in a militant society (and what is feudal society if not militant?) the position of woman is necessarily low, improving only as society becomes more industrial. The military class in Japan was restricted to the samurai, comprising nearly two million souls. Above them were the military nobles, the *daimio*, and the court nobles, the *kugé* – these higher, sybaritical nobles being fighters only in name. Below them were masses of the common people – mechanics, tradesmen, and peasants – whose life was devoted to arts of peace. Thus what Herbert Spencer gives as the characteristics of a militant type of society may be said to have been exclusively confined to the samurai class, while those of the industrial type were applicable to the classes above and below it. This is well illustrated by the position of woman; for in no class did she experience less freedom than among the samurai. Strange to say, the lower the social class – as, for instance, among small artisans – the more equal was the position of husband and wife. Among the higher nobility, too, the difference in the relations of the sexes was less marked, chiefly because there were few occasions to bring the differences of sex into prominence, the leisurely nobleman having become literally effeminate. Thus Spencer's dictum was fully exemplified in Old Japan.

I shall be guilty of gross injustice to historical truth if my words give one a very low opinion of the status of woman under Bushido. I do not hesitate to state that she was not treated as man's equal; but, until we learn to discriminate between differences and inequalities, there will always be misunderstandings upon this subject.

In view of the manifold variety of requisites for making each sex fulfil its earthly mission, the standard to be adopted in measuring its relative position must be of a composite character; or to borrow from economic language, it must be a multiple standard. Bushido had a standard of its own and it was binomial. It tried to gauge the value of woman on the battlefield and by the hearth. There she counted for very little; here for all. The treatment accorded her corresponded to this double measurement – as a social-political unit not much, while as wife and mother she received highest respect and deepest affection. While fathers and husbands were absent in field or camp, the government of the household was left entirely in the hands of mothers and wives. The education of the young, even their defence, was entrusted to them. The warlike exercises of women, of which I have spoken, were primarily to enable them intelligently to direct and follow the education of their children.

I have noticed a rather superficial notion prevailing among half-informed foreigners, that because the common Japanese expression for one's wife is 'my rustic wife' and the like, she is despised and held in little esteem. When it is told that such phrases as 'my foolish father,' 'my swinish son,' 'my awkward self,' etc., are in current use, is not the answer clear enough?

To me it seems that our idea of marital union goes in some ways farther than the so-called Christian. 'Man and woman shall be one flesh.' The individualism of the Anglo-Saxon cannot let go of the idea that husband and wife are two persons; hence when they disagree, their separate rights are recognized, and when they agree, they exhaust their vocabulary in all sorts of silly pet-names and nonsensical blandishments. It sounds highly irrational to our ears, when a husband or wife speaks to a third party of his or her other half – better or worse – as being lovely, bright, kind, and what not. Is it good taste to speak of one's self as 'my bright self,' 'my lovely disposition,' and so forth? We think praising one's own wife is praising a part of one's own self, and self-praise is regarded, to say the least, as bad taste among us – and I hope, among Christian nations too! I have diverged at some length because the polite debasement of one's consort was a usage most in vogue among the samurai.

The Teutonic races beginning their tribal life with a superstitious awe of the fair sex, and the Americans beginning their social life under the painful consciousness of the numerical insufficiency of women[29] (who, now increasing, are, I am afraid, fast losing the prestige their colonial mothers enjoyed), the respect man pays to woman has in Western civilization become the chief standard of morality. But in the martial ethics of Bushido, the main watershed dividing the good and the bad was sought elsewhere. It was located along the line of duty which bound man to his own divine soul and then to other souls in the five relations I have mentioned in the early part of this paper. Of these, we have brought to our reader's notice loyalty, the relation between one man as vassal and another as lord. Upon the rest, I have only dwelt incidentally as occasion presented itself; because they were not peculiar to Bushido. Being founded on natural affections, they could but be common to all mankind, though in some particulars they may have been accentuated by conditions which its teachings induced.

It is not surprising, however, that the virtues and teachings unique in the Precepts of Knighthood did not remain circumscribed to the military class. This makes us hasten to the consideration of the influence of Bushido on the nation at large.

CHAPTER FIFTEEN

The Influence of Bushido

Thus far we have brought into view only a few of the more prominent peaks which rise above the range of knightly virtues, in themselves so much more elevated than the general level of our national life. As the sun in its rising first tips the highest peaks with russet hue, and then gradually casts its rays on the valley below, so the ethical system which first enlightened the military order drew in course of time followers from amongst the masses. Democracy raises up a natural prince for its leader, and aristocracy infuses a princely spirit among the people. Virtues are no less contagious than vices. 'There needs but one wise man in a company, and all are wise, so rapid is the contagion,' says Emerson. No social class or caste can resist the diffusive power of moral influence.

Prate as we may of the triumphant march of Anglo-Saxon liberty, rarely has it received impetus from the masses. Was it not rather the work of the squires and *gentlemen*? Very truly does M. Taine say, 'These three syllables, as used across the channel, summarize the history of English society.' Democracy may make self-confident retorts to such a statement and fling back the question – 'When Adam delved and Eve span, where then was the gentleman?' All the more pity that a gentleman was not present in Eden! The first parents missed him sorely and paid a high price for his absence.

What Japan was she owed to the samurai. They were not only the flower of the nation, but its root as well. All the gracious gifts of Heaven flowed through them. Though they kept themselves socially aloof from the populace, they set a moral standard for them and guided them by their example. I admit Bushido had its esoteric and exoteric teachings; these were eudemonic, looking after the welfare and happiness of the commonalty; those were aretaic, emphasizing the practice of virtues for their own sake.

In the most chivalrous days of Europe, knights formed numerically but a small fraction of the population, but, as Emerson says, 'In English literature half

the drama and all the novels, from Sir Philip Sidney to Sir Walter Scott, paint this figure (gentleman).' Write in place of Sidney and Scott, Chikamatsu and Bakin, and you have in a nutshell the main features of the literary history of Japan.

The innumerable avenues of popular amusement and instruction – the theatres, the story-tellers' booths, the preacher's dais, the musical recitations, the novels – have taken for their chief theme the stories of the samurai. The peasants around the open fire in their huts never tire of repeating the achievements of

Yoshitsuné and his faithful retainer Benkéi, or of the two brave Soga brothers; the dusky urchins listen with gaping mouths until the last stick burns out and the fire dies in its embers, still leaving their hearts aglow with the tale that is told. The clerks and the shop boys, after their day's work is over and the *amado*[30] of the store are closed, gather together to relate the story of Nobunaga and Hidéyoshi far into the night, until slumber overtakes their weary eyes and transports them from the drudgery of the counter to the exploits of the field. The very babe just beginning to toddle is taught to lisp the adventures of Momotaro, the daring conqueror of ogreland. Even girls are so imbued with the love of knightly deeds and virtues that, like Desdemona, they would seriously incline to devour with greedy ear the romance of the samurai.

The samurai grew to be the *beau ideal* of the whole race. 'As among flowers the cherry is queen, so among men the samurai is lord,' so sang the populace. Debarred from commercial pursuits, the military class itself did not aid commerce; but there was no channel of human activity, no avenue of thought, which did not receive in some measure an impetus from Bushido. Intellectual and moral Japan was directly or indirectly the work of Knighthood.

How the spirit of Bushido permeated all social classes is also shown in the development of a certain order of men, known as *otoko-daté*, the natural leaders of democracy. Staunch fellows were they, every inch of them strong with the strength of massive manhood. At once the spokesmen and the guardians of popular rights, they had each a following of hundreds and thousands of souls who proffered, in the same fashion that samurai did to *daimio*, the willing service of 'limb and life, of body, chattels, and earthly honour.' Backed by a vast multitude of rash and impetuous working men, these born 'bosses' formed a formidable check to the rampancy of the two-sworded order.

In manifold ways has Bushido filtered down from the social class where it originated, and acted as leaven among the masses, furnishing a moral standard for the whole people. The Precepts of Knighthood, begun at first as the glory of the elite, became in time an aspiration and inspiration to the nation at large; and though the populace could not attain the moral height of those loftier souls, yet *Yamato Damashii*, the Soul of Japan, ultimately came to express the *Volksgeist* of the Island Realm. If religion is no more than 'Morality touched by emotion,' as

Matthew Arnold defines it, few ethical systems are better entitled to the rank of religion than Bushido. Motoöri has put the mute utterance of the nation into words when he sings:

> 'Isles of blest Japan!
> Should your Yamato spirit
> Strangers seek to scan,
> Say – scenting morn's sunlit air,
> Blows the cherry wild and fair!'

Yes, the *sakura*[31] has for ages been the favourite of our people and the emblem of our character. Mark particularly the terms of definition which the poet uses, the words *the wild cherry flower scenting the morning sun.*

The Yamato spirit is not a tame, tender plant, but a wild – in the sense of natural – growth; it is indigenous to the soil; its accidental qualities it may share with the flowers of other lands, but in its essence it remains the original, spontaneous outgrowth of our clime. But its nativity is not its sole claim to our affection. The refinement and grace of its beauty appeal to our aesthetic sense as no other flower can. We cannot share the admiration of the Europeans for their roses, which lack the simplicity of our flower. Then, too, the thorns that are hidden beneath the sweetness of the rose, the tenacity with which she clings to life, as though loth or afraid to die rather than drop untimely, preferring to rot on her stem; her showy colours and heavy odours – all these are traits so unlike our flower, which carries no dagger or poison under its beauty, which is ever ready to depart life at the call of nature, whose colours are never gorgeous, and whose light fragrance never palls. Beauty of colour and of form is limited in its showing; it is a fixed quality of existence, whereas fragrance is volatile, ethereal as the breathing of life. So in all religious ceremonies frankincense and myrrh play a prominent part. There is something spirituelle in redolence. When the delicious perfume of the sakura quickens the morning air, as the sun in its course rises to illumine first the isles of the Far East, few sensations are more serenely exhilarating than to inhale, as it were, the very breath of beauteous day.

When the Creator Himself is pictured as making new resolutions in His heart upon smelling a sweet savour (Gen. 8:21), is it any wonder that the sweet-smelling season of the cherry blossom should call forth the whole nation from their little habitations? Blame them not, if for a time their limbs forget their toil and moil and their hearts their pangs and sorrows. Their brief pleasure ended, they return to their daily task with new strength and new resolutions. Thus in ways more than one is the sakura the flower of the nation.

Is, then, this flower, so sweet and evanescent, blown whithersoever the wind listeth, and, shedding a puff of perfume, ready to vanish forever, is this flower the type of the Yamato-spirit? Is the soul of Japan so frailly mortal?

CHAPTER SIXTEEN

Is Bushido Still Alive?

Has Western civilization, in its march through our land, already wiped out every trace of its ancient discipline? It were a sad thing if a nation's soul could die so fast. That were a poor soul that could succumb so easily to extraneous influences.

The aggregate of psychological elements which constitute a national character is as tenacious as the 'irreducible elements of species, of the fins of the fish, of the beak of the bird, of the tooth of the carnivorous animal.' In his recent book, full of shallow asseverations and brilliant generalizations, M. LeBon[32] says: 'The discoveries due to the intelligence are the common patrimony of humanity; qualities or defects of character constitute the exclusive patrimony of each people: they are the firm rock which the waters must wash day by day for centuries before they can wear away even its external asperities.' These are strong words and would be highly worth pondering over, provided there were qualities and defects of character which *constitute the exclusive patrimony* of each people. Schematizing theories of this sort had been advanced long before LeBon began to write his book, and they were exploded long ago by Theodor Waitz and Hugh Murray. In studying the various virtues instilled by Bushido, we have drawn upon European sources for comparison and illustrations, and we have seen that no one quality of character was its *exclusive patrimony*. It is true the aggregate of moral qualities presents a quite unique aspect. It is this aggregate which Emerson names a 'compound result into which every

great force enters as an ingredient.' But, instead of making it, as LeBon does, an exclusive patrimony of a race or people, the Concord philosopher calls it 'an element which unites the most forcible persons of every country; makes them intelligible and agreeable to each other; and is somewhat so precise that it is at once felt if an individual lack the Masonic sign.'

The character which Bushido stamped on our nation and on the samurai in particular, cannot be said to form 'an irreducible element of species,' but nevertheless as to the vitality which it retains there is no doubt. Were Bushido a mere physical force, the momentum it has gained in the last seven hundred years could not stop so abruptly. Were it transmitted only by heredity, its influence must be immensely widespread. Just think, as M. Cheysson, a French economist, has calculated, that, supposing there be three generations in a century, 'each of us would have in his veins the blood of at least twenty millions of the people living in the year AD 1000.' The merest peasant that grubs the soil, 'bowed by the weight of centuries,' has in his veins the blood of ages, and is thus brother to us as much as 'to the ox.'

An unconscious and irresistible power, Bushido has been moving the nation and individuals. It was an honest confession of the race when Yoshida Shôin, one of the most brilliant pioneers of Modern Japan, wrote on the eve of his execution the following stanza:

> 'Full well I knew this course must end in death;
> It was Yamato spirit urged me on
> To dare whate'er betide.'

Unformulated, Bushido was and still is the animating spirit, the motor force of our country.

Mr. Ransome says that 'there are three distinct Japans in existence side by side today – the old, which has not wholly died out; the new, hardly yet born except in spirit; and the transition, passing now through its most critical throes.' While this is very true in most respects, and particularly as regards tangible and concrete institutions, the statement, as applied to fundamental ethical notions, requires some modification; for Bushido, the maker and product of Old Japan, is still the guiding principle of the transition and will prove the formative force of the new era.

The great statesmen who steered the ship of our state through the hurricane of the Restoration and the whirlpool of national rejuvenation, were men who knew no other moral teaching than the Precepts of Knighthood. Some writers[33] have lately tried to prove that the Christian missionaries contributed an appreciable quota to the making of New Japan. I would fain render honour to whom honour is due; but this honour can as yet hardly be accorded to the good missionaries. More fitting it will be to their profession to stick to the scriptural injunction of preferring one another in honour, than to advance a claim in which they have no proofs to back them. For myself, I believe that Christian missionaries are doing great things for Japan – in the domain of education, and especially of moral education: – only, the mysterious though not the less certain working of the Spirit is still hidden in divine secrecy. Whatever they do is still of indirect effect. No, as yet Christian missions have effected but little visible in moulding the character of New Japan. No, it was Bushido, pure and simple, that urged us on for weal or woe. Open the biographies of the makers of Modern Japan – of Sakuma, of Saigo, of Okubo, of Kido, not to mention the reminiscences of living men such as Ito, Okuma, Itagaki, etc. – and you will find that it was under the impetus of samuraihood that they thought and wrought. When Mr. Henry Norman declared, after his study and observation of the Far East, that the only respect in which Japan differed from other oriental despotisms lay in 'the ruling influence among her people of the strictest, loftiest, and the most punctilious codes of honour that man has ever devised,' he touched the mainspring which has made New Japan what she is, and which will make her what she is destined to be.[34]

The transformation of Japan is a fact patent to the whole world. Into a work of such magnitude various motives naturally entered; but if one were to name the principal, one would not hesitate to name Bushido. When we opened the whole country to foreign trade, when we introduced the latest improvements in every department of life, when we began to study Western politics and sciences, our guiding motive was not the development of our physical resources and the increase of wealth; much less was it a blind imitation of Western customs.

A close observer of oriental institutions and peoples has written:

> 'We are told every day how Europe has influenced Japan, and forget that the change in those islands was entirely self-generated, that Europeans did not teach Japan, but that Japan of herself chose to learn from Europe methods of organization, civil and military, which have so far proved successful. She imported European mechanical science, as the Turks years before imported European artillery. That is not exactly influence,' continues Mr. Townsend, 'unless, indeed, England is influenced by purchasing tea in China. Where is the European apostle,' asks our author, 'or philosopher or statesman or agitator, who has re-made Japan?'[35]

Mr. Townsend has well perceived that the spring of action which brought about the changes in Japan lay entirely within our own selves; and if he had only probed into our psychology, his keen powers of observation would easily have convinced him that this spring was no other than Bushido. The sense of honour which cannot bear being looked down upon as an inferior power – that was the strongest of motives. Pecuniary or industrial considerations were awakened later in the process of transformation.

The influence of Bushido is still so palpable that he who runs may read. A glimpse into Japanese life will make it manifest. Read Hearn, the most eloquent and truthful interpreter of the Japanese mind, and you see the working of that mind to be an example of the working of Bushido. The universal politeness of the people, which is the legacy of knightly ways, is too well known to be repeated anew. The physical endurance, fortitude, and bravery that 'the little Jap' possesses, were sufficiently proved in the Chino-Japanese war.[36] 'Is there any nation more loyal and patriotic?' is a question asked by many; and for the proud answer, 'There is not,' we must thank the Precepts of Knighthood.

On the other hand, it is fair to recognize that for the very faults and defects of our character, Bushido is largely responsible. Our lack of abstruse philosophy – while some of our young men have already gained international reputation in scientific researches, not one has achieved anything in philosophical lines – is traceable to the neglect of metaphysical training under Bushido's regimen of education. Our sense of honour is responsible for our exaggerated sensitiveness and touchiness; and if there is the conceit in us with which some foreigners charge us, that, too, is a pathological outcome of honour.

Deep-rooted and powerful as is still the effect of Bushido, I have said that it is an unconscious and mute influence. The heart of the people responds, without knowing a reason why, to any appeal made to what it has inherited, and hence the same moral idea expressed in a newly translated term and in an old Bushido term, has a vastly different degree of efficacy. A backsliding Christian, whom no pastoral persuasion could help from downward tendency, was reverted from his course by an appeal made to his loyalty, the fidelity he once swore to his Master. The word 'Loyalty' revived all the noble sentiments that were permitted to grow lukewarm. A party of unruly youths engaged in a long-continued 'students' strike' in a college, on account of their dissatisfaction with a certain teacher, disbanded at two simple questions put by the Director – 'Is your professor a worthy character? If so, you ought to respect him and keep him in the school. Is he weak? If so, it is not manly to push a falling man.' The scientific incapacity of the professor, which was the beginning of the trouble, dwindled into insignificance in comparison with the moral issues hinted at. By arousing the sentiments nurtured by Bushido, moral renovation of great magnitude can be accomplished.

One cause of the failure of mission work is that most of the missionaries are entirely ignorant of our history – 'What do we care for heathen records?' some say – and consequently estrange their religion from the habits of thought we and our forefathers have been accustomed to for centuries past. Mocking a nation's history? – as though the career of any people even of the lowest African savages possessing no record – were not a page in the general history of mankind, written by the hand of God Himself. Ignoring the past career of a people, missionaries claim that Christianity is a new religion, whereas, to my mind, it is an 'old, old story,' which, if presented in intelligible words – that is to say, if expressed in the vocabulary familiar in the moral development of a people – will find easy lodgment in their hearts, irrespective of race or nationality. Christianity in its American or English form – with more of Anglo-Saxon freaks and fancies than grace and purity of its Founder – is a poor scion to graft on Bushido stock. Should the propagator of the new faith uproot the

entire stock, root, and branches, and plant the seeds of the Gospel on the ravaged soil? Such a heroic process may be possible – in Hawaii, where, it is alleged, the Church militant had complete success in amassing spoils of wealth itself, and in annihilating the aboriginal race; such a process is most decidedly impossible in Japan – nay, it is a process which Jesus Himself would never have adopted in founding His kingdom on earth.

It behoves us to take more to heart the following words of a saintly man, devout Christian, and profound scholar:

> 'Men have divided the world into heathen and Christian, without considering how much good may have been hidden in the one or how much evil may have been mingled with the other. They have compared the best part of themselves with the worst of their neighbours, the ideal of Christianity with the corruption of Greece or of the East. They have not aimed at impartiality, but have been contented to accumulate all that could be said in praise of their own, and in dispraise of other forms of religion.'[37]

But, whatever may be the error committed by individuals, there is little doubt that the fundamental principle of the religion they profess is a power which we must take into account in reckoning the future of Bushido, whose days seem to be already numbered. Ominous signs are in the air that betoken its future. Not only signs, but redoubtable forces are at work to threaten it.

CHAPTER SEVENTEEN

The Future of Bushido

Few historical comparisons can be more judiciously made than between the Chivalry of Europe and the Bushido of Japan, and, if history repeats itself, it certainly will do with the fate of the latter what it did with that of the former. The particular and local causes for the decay of chivalry which St. Palaye gives, have, of course, little application to Japanese conditions; but the larger and more general causes that helped to undermine knighthood and chivalry in and after the Middle Ages are as surely working for the decline of Bushido.

One remarkable difference between the experience of Europe and of Japan is, that whereas in Europe, when chivalry was weaned from feudalism and was adopted by the Church, it obtained a fresh lease of life, in Japan no religion was large enough to nourish it; hence, when the mother institution, feudalism, was gone, Bushido, left an orphan, had to shift for itself. The present elaborate military organization might take it under its patronage, but we know that modern warfare can afford little room for its continuous growth. Shintoism, which fostered it in its infancy, is itself superannuated. The hoary sages of ancient China are being supplanted by the intellectual parvenu of the type of Bentham and Mill. Moral theories of a comfortable kind, flattering to the Chauvinistic tendencies of the time, and therefore thought well adapted to the need of this day, have been invented and propounded; but as yet we hear only their shrill voices echoing through the columns of yellow journalism.

Principalities and powers are arrayed against the Precepts of Knighthood. Already, as Veblen says, 'the decay of the ceremonial code – or, as it is otherwise called, the vulgarization of life – among the industrial classes proper, has become one of the chief enormities of latter-day civilization in the eyes of all persons of delicate sensibilities.' The irresistible tide of triumphant democracy, which can tolerate no form or shape of trust – and Bushido was a trust organized by those who monopolized reserve capital of intellect and culture, fixing the grades and value of moral qualities – is alone powerful enough to engulf the remnant of Bushido. The present societary forces are antagonistic to petty class spirit, and chivalry is, as Freeman severely criticizes, a class spirit. Modern society, if it pretends to any unity, cannot admit 'purely personal obligations devised in the interests of an exclusive class.'[38] Add to this the progress of popular instruction, of industrial arts and habits, of wealth and city-life – then we can easily see that neither the keenest cuts of samurai sword nor the sharpest shafts shot from Bushido's boldest bows can aught avail. The state built upon the rock of Honour and fortified by the same – shall we call it the *Ehrenstaat*, or, after the manner of Carlyle, the Heroarchy? – is fast falling into the hands of quibbling lawyers and gibbering politicians armed with logic-chopping engines of war. The words which a great thinker used in speaking of Theresa and Antigone may aptly be repeated of the samurai, that 'the medium in which their ardent deeds took shape is forever gone.'

Alas for knightly virtues! alas for samurai pride! Morality ushered into the world with the sound of bugles and drums, is destined to fade away as 'the captains and the kings depart.'

If history can teach us anything, the state built on martial virtues – be it a city like Sparta or an Empire like Rome – can never make on earth a 'continuing city.' Universal and natural as is the fighting instinct in man, fruitful as it has proved to be of noble sentiments and manly virtues, it does not comprehend the whole man. Beneath the instinct to fight there lurks a diviner instinct – to love. We have seen that Shintoism, Mencius, and Wan Yang Ming, have all clearly taught it; but Bushido and all other militant types of ethics, engrossed doubtless, with questions of immediate practical need, too often forgot duly to emphasize this fact. Life has grown larger in these latter times. Callings nobler and broader than a warrior's claim our attention today. With an enlarged view of life, with the growth of democracy, with better knowledge of other peoples and nations, the Confucian idea of benevolence – dare I also add the Buddhist idea of pity? – will expand into the Christian conception of love. Men have become more than subjects, having grown to the estate of citizens; nay, they are more than citizens – being men. Though war clouds hang heavy upon our horizon, we will believe that the wings of the angel of peace can disperse them. The history of the world confirms the prophecy that 'the meek shall inherit the earth.' A nation that sells its birthright of peace, and backslides from the front rank of industrialism into the file of filibusterism, makes a poor bargain indeed!

When the conditions of society are so changed that they have become not only adverse but hostile to Bushido, it is time for it to prepare for an honourable burial. It is just as difficult to point out when chivalry dies, as to determine the exact time of its inception. Dr. Miller says that chivalry was formally abolished in the year 1559, when Henry II of France was slain in a tournament. With us, the edict formally abolishing feudalism in 1870 was the signal to toll the knell of Bushido. The edict, issued five years later, prohibiting the wearing of swords, rang out the old, 'the unbought grace of life, the cheap defence of nations, the nurse of manly sentiment and heroic enterprise,' it rang in the new age of 'sophisters, economists, and calculators.'

It has been said that Japan won her late war with China[39] by means of Murata guns and Krupp cannon; it has been said the victory was the work of a modern school-system; but these are less than half-truths. Does ever a piano, be it of the choicest workmanship of Ehrbar or Steinway burst forth into the Rhapsodies of Liszt or the Sonatas of Beethoven, without a master's hand? Or, if guns win battles, why did not Louis Napoleon beat the Prussians with his *Mitrailleuse*, or the Spaniards with their Mausers the Filipinos, whose arms were no better than the old-fashioned Remingtons? Needless to repeat what has grown a trite saying – that it is the spirit that quickeneth, without which the best of implements profiteth but little. The most improved guns and cannon do not shoot of their own accord; the most modern educational system does not make a coward a hero. No! What won the battles on the Yalu, in Korea and Manchuria, were the ghosts of our fathers, guiding our hands and beating in our hearts. They are not dead, those ghosts, the spirits of our warlike ancestors. To those who have eyes to see, they are clearly visible. Scratch a Japanese of the most advanced ideas, and he will show a samurai. The great inheritance of honour, of valour, and of all martial virtues is, as Professor Cramb very fitly expresses it, 'but ours on trust, the fief inalienable of the dead and of the generations to come,' and the summons of the present is to guard this heritage, nor to bate one jot of the ancient spirit; the summons of the future will be so to widen its scope as to apply it in all walks and relations of life.

It has been predicted – and predictions have been corroborated by the events of the last half-century – that the moral system of Feudal Japan, like its castles and its armouries, will crumble into dust, and new ethics rise phoenix-like to lead New Japan in her path of progress. Desirable and probable as the fulfilment of such a prophecy is, we must not forget that a phoenix rises only from its own ashes, and that it is not a bird of passage, neither does it fly on pinions borrowed from other birds. 'The Kingdom of God is within you.' It does not come rolling down the mountains, however lofty; it does not come sailing across the seas, however broad. 'God has granted,' says the Koran, 'to every people a prophet in

its own tongue.' The seeds of the Kingdom, as vouched for and apprehended by the Japanese mind, blossomed in Bushido. Now its days are closing – sad to say, before its full fruition – and we turn in every direction for other sources of sweetness and light, of strength and comfort, but among them there is as yet nothing found to take its place.

Bushido as an independent code of ethics may vanish, but its power will not perish from the earth; its schools of martial prowess or civic honour may be demolished, but its light and its glory will long survive their ruins. Like its symbolic flower, after it is blown to the four winds, it will still bless mankind with the perfume with which it will enrich life. Ages after, when its customaries will have been buried and its very name forgotten, its odours will come floating in the air as from a far-off, unseen hill, 'the wayside gaze beyond'; – then in the beautiful language of the Quaker poet,

> *'The traveller owns the grateful sense*
> *Of sweetness near, he knows not whence,*
> *And, pausing, takes with forehead bare*
> *The benediction of the air.'*

Endnotes

1　Pronounced *Boó-shee-doh*.

2　*History Philosophically Illustrated*, (3rd Edition, 1853), Volume 2, page 2.

3　Lafcadio Hearn, *Exotics and Retrospectives*, page 84.

4　*The English People*, page 188.

5　*Feudal and Modern Japan*, Volume 1, page 183.

6　Miwa Shissai.

7　Burke, *French Revolution*.

8　'These shall be thy arts: to impose the law of peace, / To spare the conquered, and to defeat the proud.' From *Aeneid VI*, Virgil (Ed.)

9　A musical instrument, resembling the guitar.

10　The *uguisu* or warbler, sometimes called the nightingale of Japan.

11　Literally 'well–seatedness.'

12　Hanging scrolls, which may be either paintings or ideograms, used for decorative purposes.

13　Peery, *The Gist of Japan*, p. 86.

14　*Philosophy of History* (English translation by Sibree), Part 4, section 2, chapter 1.

15　In 1894 Alfred Dreyfus, a Jewish captain in the French army, was falsely convicted of treason for espionage and exiled to a penal colony. When the real culprit came to light, the military authorities refused to exonerate Dreyfus, leading to accusations of anti-Semitism and a full-blown political furore that exposed deep political divisions in the French Republic. (Ed.)

16 *Religions of Japan.*

17 *Principles of Ethics,* Vol. 1, Part 2, chapter 10.

18 The same word as that misspelled jiu-jitsu in common English parlance. It is the gentle art. It 'uses no weapon.'

19 'Learn to suffer without complaint.' (Ed.)

20 Edwin Arnold.

21 Seated himself – that is, in the Japanese fashion, his knees and toes touching the ground and his body resting on his heels. In this position, which is one of respect, he remained until his death.

22 I use Dr. Legge's translation verbatim.

23 Morselli, *Suicide*, page 314.

24 *Suicide and Insanity.*

25 The game of *go* is sometimes called Japanese checkers, but is much more intricate than the English game. The *go*-board contains 361 squares and is supposed to represent a battle-field – the object of the game being to occupy as much space as possible.

26 Kitchen, Church, Children. (Ed.)

27 Lecky, *History of European Morals*, 2, page 383.

28 For a very sensible explanation of nudity and bathing see Finck's *Lotos Time in Japan*, pages 286–97.

29 I refer to those days when girls were imported from England and given in marriage for so many pounds of tobacco, etc.

30 Outside shutters.

31 *Cerasus pseudo-cerasus*, Lindley.

32 *The Psychology of Peoples*, page 33.

33 Speer: *Missions and Politics in Asia*, Lecture 4, pages 189–92; Dennis: *Christian Missions and Social Progress*, Volume 1, page 32, Volume 2, page 70 etc.

34 *The Far East*, page 375.

35 Meredith Townsend, *Asia and Europe*, page 28.

36 Among other works on the subject, read Eastlake and Yamada on *Heroic Japan*, and Diosy on *The New Far East*.

37 Jowett, *Sermons on Faith and Doctrine*, 2.

38 *Norman Conquest*, Volume 5, page 482.

39 The First Sino-Japanese War, 1894–5. (Ed.)